JAMES JOYCE TODAY
ESSAYS ON THE MAJOR WORKS

COMMEMORATING THE TWENTY-FIFTH ANNIVERSARY OF HIS DEATH

JAMES JOYCE TODAY
ESSAYS ON THE MAJOR WORKS

*Edited
with a Preface
by
Thomas F. Staley*

GREENWOOD PRESS, PUBLISHERS
WESTPORT, CONNECTICUT

Library of Congress Cataloging in Publication Data
Staley, Thomas F   ed.
  James Joyce today.

  Reprint of the ed. published by Indiana University
Press, Bloomington.
  Includes bibliographical references.
  CONTENTS: Kelly, R. G. Joyce hero.--Howarth, H.
Chamber music and its place in the Joyce canon.--
Atherton, J. S. The Joyce of Dubliners.--[etc.]
  1. Joyce, James, 1882-1941--Criticism and inter-
pretation--Addresses, essays, lectures. I. Title.
[PR6019.O9Z812 1979]   823'.9'12   79-17222
ISBN 0-313-21292-9

Copyright © 1966 by Indiana University Press

All rights reserved

No part of this book may be reproduced or utilized in any form or
by any means, electronic or mechanical, including photocopying,
recording, or by any information storage and retrieval system, without
permission in writing from the Publisher.

First published in 1966 by Indiana University Press, Bloomington,
Indiana

Reprinted with the permission of Indiana University Press

Reprinted in 1979 by Greenwood Press, Inc.
51 Riverside Avenue, Westport, CT 06880

Printed in the United States of America

10 9 8 7 6 5 4 3 2 1

Contents

	Preface by Thomas F. Staley	vii
1.	Introduction JOYCE HERO by Robert Glynn Kelly	3
2.	CHAMBER MUSIC AND ITS PLACE IN THE JOYCE CANON by Herbert Howarth	11
3.	THE JOYCE OF DUBLINERS by James S. Atherton	28
4.	A PORTRAIT OF THE ARTIST AS A YOUNG MAN: AFTER FIFTY YEARS by William T. Noon, S.J.	54
5.	THE POSITION OF ULYSSES TODAY by Richard M. Kain	83
6.	JAMES JOYCE IN THE SMITHY OF HIS SOUL by William Blissett	96
7.	FINNEGANS WAKE IN PERSPECTIVE by Clive Hart	135
	Notes	167
	Biographical Notes	182

Preface

Ironically, when James Joyce died in Zurich twenty-five years ago (1941) at the age of fifty-nine, the announcement—largely because of the war—produced small reverberation in the literary world. The irony lies, of course, in the fact that virtually no writer since has had more serious scholarly attention paid to him: though his first known work appeared in 1901, so far the 1960 decade-in-progress alone has seen over thirty books and more than five hundred articles devoted to Joyce's life and works. In spite of great specialization within this crescendo of studies (on such topics as influences, style, technique, themes, biography), the immense total bears testimony to the fact that Joyce has still a meaningful hold upon our time.

It is fitting, then, on the twenty-fifth anniversary of his death, to survey for new generations of students as well as for seasoned readers the present status of Joyce. The essays which follow, by mature and productive scholars assessing his major works from one point of view and another, are arranged in the chronological order in which the books themselves appeared, thereby bringing into view Joyce's creative life in its successive stages.

In an introduction entitled "Joyce Hero" Robert Glynn Kelly shows Joyce in relation to his critic-reader. Herbert Howarth in *"Chamber Music* and Its Place in the Joyce Canon" views Joyce's collection of verse from the perspective of *A Portrait of the Artist as a Young Man* and *Ulysses.* "The Joyce of *Dubliners"* presents an account of James Atherton's exploration into the style, structure, and writing technique in Joyce's volume of short stories, and views *Dubliners* in the light of Joyce's later creative work. William T. Noon, S.J., centers most of his essay *"A Portrait of the Artist as a Young Man:* After Fifty Years" upon Stephen Dedalus, the hero of *A Portrait,* and the problems surrounding the character.

More has been written about *Ulysses* than about any other single novel of our century—to appraise the scholarship would require a book-length essay—but Richard M. Kain has summarized the variety of extant opinion in his essay "The Position of *Ulysses* Today." "James Joyce in the Smithy of His Soul" by William Blissett offers important insight into Stephen Dedalus, as it also shows the influence of Wagner upon Joyce.

The final essay, Clive Hart's *"Finnegans Wake* in Perspective," is conceived in such form as to give readers courage to take the rational approach to the conundrum of *Finnegan,* which, likely always to remain at least partially a mystery, readers will always feel under compulsion to solve.

THOMAS F. STALEY

July, 1966

JAMES JOYCE TODAY
ESSAYS ON THE MAJOR WORKS

1

Introduction

JOYCE HERO

Robert Glynn Kelly

James Joyce planned his career with such care and thoroughness he even planned his critics. He devised all sorts of puzzles expressly for them, he scheduled the solutions to these puzzles (when the critics fell behind schedule, he issued clues), and he buried with surpassing skill the things he wanted the critics never to discover. Thus even today when we come up with a new insight into Joyce we may have the uncomfortable feeling that we are just carrying out an assignment, just bringing back from the garden one more numbered package Joyce planted there long ago. Certainly there is no other author who himself knew perfectly well the answers to so many of the questions his critics are trying to answer.

Frank O'Connor, noting that the characters in his own short stories often manifest a stubborn willfulness when he tries to tell them what to do, opines that none of the characters in *Dubliners* ever talked back to Joyce. Nor do his readers. Nor, very often, do his critics. There is a strikingly small percentage of appraisal in Joyce criticism—partially because the critics are intimidated and partially because Joyce has given them so much other work to do—easier work, on the whole, surer work, work largely without risk and apparently without end. It is risky to appraise the latest outrageous gesture of a man whose earlier outrageous gestures are now accepted as literary triumphs—even if the latest gesture seems more outrageous than all the others. The trouble is, the man has been every bit as good as he is at present outrageous. His unquestionable greatness balances his apparent outrageousness to an exact, perilous ambiguity. Notoriously, no critic wants to be a later version of the critic who killed Keats. Still less does he want to ride at mastodon-Joyce with a lance that may turn out to be a straw.

All this implies that Joyce wrote with the critic-reader (it is clear that even in regard to Joyce's earliest work critic and reader are really one; you can't disjoin them without losing blood) very much in mind. He did. This does not mean that he ever wrote *for* the reader, compromising on his behalf. Joyce never compromised. An artistic task was for him an equation to be solved absolutely on its own terms. But the critic-reader was inevitably one of those terms. Joyce never simply expressed himself, pouring out his soul in a thoughtless rapture. He contrived intricate and precise literary effects. He meant those effects to take place in the reader's mind. He could therefore no more afford to be mistaken about that mind than he could afford to be mistaken about any other term of the equation. He had to meet the reader at some point, even if he meant thereafter to lead him where he never could have imagined going at the outset. This is why, for all his arrogant independence and what his brother called an "indifference to obloquy [that] surpassed belief," Joyce was truly disturbed when his audience failed to respond properly. He worried much that he had missed his mark. His critics perhaps don't worry enough.

But Joyce himself was a major term of the equation too, and never was a personality more providentially designed for the literary critics. Just by being true to himself, Joyce made endless fodder for them. He had, first of all, an absolute reverence for fact. What existed, all the disparate things that had happened (and were thus "lodged in the room of the infinite possibilities they [had] ousted") were for him sacred—every bit as sacred as they were for Hopkins, for whom they were all direct expressions of God. (Perhaps they were for Joyce, too.) Furthermore, Joyce, as he himself put it, lacked imagination. He could not invent, he would only elaborate, develop, build up what was already there. "Have you ever noticed," he said to Frank Budgen, "when you get an idea, how much *I* can make of it?" (Note how nicely his ego survives his self-criticism.) Thus into his books went actual faces and names and streets and buildings and an astonishing number of word-for-word statements and other intact fragments, and these in turn were arranged in accordance with schemes and structures and even specific scenes and paragraph-rhythms borrowed from other literary works or from the rudimentary creations of his brother and his friends. Or he structured his fictions on the highly discursive non-fictions of philosophers and theologians. All these shards and shreds are there for the critic to dig out. And since any particular fragment may have traveled, for example, from Stanislaus' conversation to Stanislaus' notebooks to Joyce's notebooks to successive stages of his work, the most humble of them can have a sufficiently complex genealogy to give the critic a fair amount of exercise.

The critic is served also by Joyce's curious dedication to symbols and correspondences, to mysticism and cabal. There was not for him a hard line between symbol and fact, or between science and superstition. Therefore the real world was far more extensive for him than for most people. Its map was thick with configurations and names which other people found fanciful and esoteric and often had to look up in books. More digging. Then there is the highly special relationship between Joyce's life and his work. He did not simply live his life and then write about it. He lived it *in order* to write about it. He stage-managed it to provide better material for his books. Though he believed the role of art was to order life, he first ordered his life so as to facilitate his art. Thus many of the symbols and themes of his work were actual obsessions in his life—obsessions (exile, persecution, betrayal) which he cultivated, at least partially, as a beggar cultivates an affliction—so that he can make a profit from it later on. More digging.

All of this digging is not necessarily profitable, but Joyce provides the critic with plenty of work that is. For all his rigid schemes and frameworks, his books are, like all true poetry, indeterminate. His frameworks may be numbered and closed, like Dante's, but his meanings are open. All his logic and all his facts are at the service of his mysticism. He said: "Beauty, the splendor of truth, is a gracious presence when the imagination contemplates intensely the truth of its own being or the visible world, and the spirit which proceeds out of truth and beauty is the holy spirit of joy. These are realities and these alone give and sustain life." And in the spirit of that statement he set about studying city directories. He said: "I mean that I am trying in my poems to give people some kind of intellectual pleasure or spiritual enjoyment by converting the bread of everyday life into something that has a permanent life of its own." And to this end he compiled statistics from the Dublin newspapers. Though he dug into facts like an Upton Sinclair, the image of his art is not reporting. It is not even poetic transcendence. It is, as he indicates above, transubstantiation. Thus, for all his furious respect for fact, he knew he could magnificently surpass it. Thus, too, he was willing to borrow, take, steal so much so shamelessly from such assorted people (Stanislaus and George Moore and Bret Harte), because he knew he could surpass them all. This strange combination of the factual and the rigorously systematic with the mystical at once guarantees that the criticism of his work will never end and offers it everywhere the solid footholds that encourage it to begin.

It is clear that Joyce, though he was dependent upon others to get his mind started, and though he clung to assorted prefabricated frameworks with what may look from one point of view like caution, ventured about as far as any artist ever did into the trackless regions of aesthetic creation. He had almost unbelievable courage. He had Keats' famous "Negative Capability"—"when a man is capable of being in uncertainties, mysteries, doubts, without any irritable reaching after fact and reason." For he worked toward an effect—something which you measure by feel and not by logic and which never offers you the security of logic. He would have delighted Coleridge by the way in which he took the fixities and definites of other men and fused them into organic, living wholes. For all his mechanics, he was no mechanic. One of the astonishing things about *Ulysses* is the fact that from all the hard discrete elements imbedded in it there arises a veritable mist of meaning. It is an ambience. It is the indeterminate effusion of real things. It has the totality of our perceptions of life before we have parcelled them out into concepts, cut them down into categories—irritably reaching after fact and reason. There stands, sounds, smells that solid city, and the fact that its life flows well beyond our limited, frantically searching senses and comes to us in sharp spurts and static prolonged pauses and varied overlapping threads which are never quite reconciled, never reduced to neat exactness and the artificial completeness of the inventory—this is the best guarantee in the world of its reality. You can respond to the meanings of *Ulysses,* feel them, see them, experience them like life itself, and if you are a good critic you can evoke them for others. But you can never define them.

The misguided critic tries to define them—or seems to. Busily digging out the hard abstractions with which Joyce began, he gives the effect of imposing these abstractions on Joyce's work. He seems to read Joyce in terms of a discursive definiteness which Joyce considered the antithesis of art. Joyce, once again, worked for an *effect*. He knew quite clearly what effect he wanted. He preferred to suppress *Stephen Hero* because he wanted the *Portrait* to function without it. But we seize upon *Stephen Hero* to throw as much light as we can into Joyce's carefully contrived shadows. We try to reduce the effect of the *Portrait* to meanings and origins—in the belief that we will then better see the effect. We may well be right. But Joyce would not agree. Similarly we would like to get our hands on that Pound-edited version of *The Waste Land*—but Eliot obviously did not agree with us either.

Yes, Joyce, no mechanic, left his meanings open. Indeed, the question is now raised as to whether he sometimes left them too far open, gave his work too much autonomy, was too opportunistic, was (he, of all people!) artistically irresponsible. The question is worth raising. Stuart Gilbert said long ago, presumably with Joyce's encouragement, that the form of *Ulysses* is such that anything and everything is relevant to it. But where everything is relevant, nothing is. When form ceases to select, it ceases to be form. It may be mysticism, but it is not art.

But the question, though worth raising, is peripheral. What matters is that most of Joyce's work is open but controlled, controlled with extraordinary firmness and yet to that delicately limited degree Keats had in mind. Joyce's work is full of a truly aesthetic potentiality on which the good critic can do himself proud.

Furthermore, amid all the necessary analysis and explication and documentation, the reader finds himself again and again driven back to the simple appreciative response. Joyce's excellence is so often intrinsic and indubitable, so often right there on the surface, so often a matter of sheer eloquence, like that of Hopkins or Yeats, that we care not how high the scholarly edifice is raised, we can always enjoy ourselves in the warm sun outside its shadow. We can come back to the works again and again, not laboring biography, for example, using it lightly at most, and always find new riches, just as we can always find new riches in Shakespeare, whose biography is fortunately lost to us. At the same time, we know the critical edifice is absolutely necessary. We have only to recall the day when the public had difficulty discerning even the *Odyssey*-parallel in *Ulysses,* or grasping the mode of aesthetic detachment in the *Portrait,* to appreciate how much Joyce criticism has done for us. Like all criticism it is both useful and dangerous—but more dangerous than the criticism of most authors.

One other obvious reason why Joyce provides such excellent and inexhaustible material for critics is that he was more than one writer. He refused ever to write the same kind of book twice. The courage and pride and intense artistic discipline of this man in whom self-indulgence, though lavish, was kept precisely in its place, led him to seek at each stage of his career not merely a new book, but a new art. He may in the end have been led a bit too far, but along the way he gave us those superbly individuated works which, while they shed light upon one another—are indeed essential to one another—never solve one another. They fall farther short of solving one another than the works of just about any other author. For this reason alone, Joyce will never yield much of himself to any one critical key or system, or to any one critic. He will never be anybody's monopoly.

Finally, Joyce serves the critic by a perfectionism which renders the least aspect of his work critically significant. All of his decisions may not be admirable, but they are all thoroughly decided. His work is finished, "done," to the last letter. There is no fringe of the casual, no mere neutral medium in which a certain percentage of significant pattern is traced, none of the anonymous tables and chairs Robert Louis Stevenson got so tired of putting into his stories. E. M. Forster has said that writing is made up of inspiration and faking—and we know what he means. Gerard Manley Hopkins divided poetry into the language of true inspiration and what he called Parnassian (good stuff but not of the best, just a bit manufactured, perhaps, a bit of chronic style)—and we know what *he* meant. But Joyce never faked and he never wrote Parnassian. He diligently and systematically worked everything up to the same high level—whatever you choose to call that level. And if you don't call it inspiration you have to admit it is usually just as good. As for the times when it is not—the apparently (eyeing the mastodon, we take no chances) excessive clowning, the puerile jokes, the wearisomely prolonged stunts—we know they too are just as fully intentioned, just as finished, as everything else and therefore call for a kind of critical attention they would not call for in another author.

There was never a more serious artist than Joyce. He accepted his own rare nature as a divine commission, a life-subsuming responsibility. He studied his own nature thoroughly and neglected none of it. This is why his variety and his excellence are both genuine. His many voices are not a ventriloquist's act. Nor are the successive experiments which supersede one another. They are all equally Joyce. A man of many parts, living therefore in a world of many parts, he tried to express all he knew, but could never get it all into one voice. He is complex and enigmatic in ways that are highly useful. Thus his work will continue to be a fair field for critics. It provides for criticism of an exceptionally various excellence. Look, for example, into the present volume.

2

CHAMBER MUSIC AND ITS PLACE IN THE JOYCE CANON

Herbert Howarth

I

The place of *Chamber Music* in the Joyce canon is at once first, last, and nowhere. Chronologically it is first. It is last for most critics. It is nowhere for most readers, who ignore it or read it too rapidly to gather what it can give. Joyce's own view, even at the moment when he had his worst doubts and almost withheld the volume from publication, was that the poems had "grace";[1] and perhaps he would also have called them "dainty," the word he uses in *A Portrait of the Artist* to describe the Elizabethan song which he sang at the piano.[2] For the historian the book is certainly and organically what Joyce allowed it to become when he quelled his doubts and let the printer proceed: Opus I; the first stage in the evolution of the complete opera.

"It is not a book of love verses at all, I perceive," Joyce wrote to his brother.[3] They are not love verses because they do not really attempt to reach a woman, to speak to her, to persuade her, nor do they really attempt to reflect their writer's experience of love or even of the fantasy of love. They are essays in style. This in two senses. They are essays in a style of life. Although they are not purely "Shakespearean" or "Jonsonian" or "lutanist" (since other influences from Horace to the Victorian drawing room ballads, from the Irish come-all-yous to Verlaine, converge in them), yet their singer takes shape, if a blurred shape, as a grave-mannered gentleman of a pre-industrial world, a courtier. Something must be said about him later. They are also essays in style in the more familiar literary meaning of the term: essays in the arrangement of words to please the ear. *Pulchra sunt quae audita placent.*

Read as an exhibition of the verbal skill, the more satisfying for the carefully-spun simplicity of the context, *Chamber Music* will seem a remarkable collection. It bears the sign which characterizes the poetic stylist in all languages, the deliberate invention of technical obligations and their fulfillment. In each stanza of Poem VIII, Joyce obliges himself to renew and amplify the first line in the third line. He loves to take a word from one stanza and employ it in the next in a different position. In Poem X he agreeably converts two rhyming nouns of the first stanza, *streamers* and *dreamers,* into two rhyming participles in the corresponding lines of the second stanza. The craft of the disposition and redisposition of words in a short lyric might be learned from *Chamber Music.* So might the art of the reduction of large-scale effects to lyric proportions. We know how Joyce was gratified by the rhetoric with which Seymour Bushe spoke of Michelangelo's Moses, the frozen music, "which, if anything that the hand of man has wrought of noble and inspiring and beautiful deserves to live deserves to live."[4] That immediate closure of a whole period by the iteration of a verb that has just closed a subordinate clause, Joyce uses and extends in *Ulysses,* and uses but appropriately curbs in *Chamber Music*—when he tells his sweetheart or his soul to repudiate the slanderers:

> They are sadder than all tears;
>   Their lives ascend as a continual sigh.
> Proudly answer to their tears:
>   As they deny, deny.

His literary architecture, metropolitan in *Ulysses* and *Finnegans Wake,* Joyce practices in miniature in *Chamber Music.* Parallel parentheses, parallel questions, hold stanza supported against stanza. Songs curve in elegant quasi-palindrome to end as they began.

There is a spice of absurdity in proving the talents of rhetoric in a writer who through the course of a lifetime was to demonstrate a master's power over the styles of his precursors and contemporaries: who was to resume the prose of all the eras of English literature in the "Deshil Holles Eamus" chapter of *Ulysses;* who parodied *The Waste Land;*[5] who dexterously plied a birthday lyric into five languages, each version authentic in tone and tune.[6] The reminder of the obvious is to clarify the intention of Opus I. The persistent stylistic care has one predominant purpose, implicit in the title of the volume. The aim is "music."

It is legitimate to call Joyce neoclassical and to see him in the neoclassical procession of our century. Yet the term is too narrow and too broad. Joyce was a Romantic poet as well as an Archaic. And of the classical centuries he totally ignored the eighteenth, for some observers the supremely classical. He was not of the Age of Reason. He valued the lyric above all other poetry, and understood its birth and its beauty as beyond the reach of reason or observation. That is clear from his love of Mangan, from his appeal to the standard of "Es war ein König in Thule,"[7] from his rejection of Meredith's poetry for its lack of the lyrical impulse.[8] In both *A Portrait* and *Ulysses* he describes Stephen writing a lyric,[9] and shows with scrupulosity of introspection that it is a brimming of unconscious powers and knowledge: that it is indeed a "spontaneous overflow of powerful feeling." It overflows as music. "A song by Shakespeare or Verlaine, which seems so free and living and as remote from any conscious purpose as rain that falls in a garden or the lights of evening, is discovered to be the rhythmic speech of an emotion otherwise incommunicable, at least so fitly."[10]

The Age of Reason judged that one of the problems of the poet was to make his sound seem an echo of the sense. Joyce worked from the opposite point. His effort was to find sense capable of carrying the sound that he heard when the inner life brimmed over. The sense must be the medium of the sound. He was a musician in search of a system of notation. When Joyce perceived that the poems of *Chamber Music* were not love poems, this was what he perceived: that he had been looking for words to register the music of the emotions of a young man of twenty-two.

The purpose was music. And the success? A partial success: the music is there for the seeking but does not invade the reader unless it is patiently sought. If we give the songs of *Chamber Music* several readings, they begin to take hold; and afterwards, when we are about other occupations, the music will stir in the memory, possibly without the accompaniment of the words; the melody will rise, fall, recur, prolong itself, offer its atmosphere and world picture.

But we do not give them so much reading, unless for a paper of this kind. And a writer is at least partly to blame if we read him no more than perfunctorily. He has not put in enough to detain the eye. What Joyce has not given to *Chamber Music* is enough sense to carry the music. For us on this North American continent at this period when some density is expected of literature, density and a scatter of potent symbols which we may construe and connect ad lib., the verses want substance. Together with his view of its music, Joyce seems to have had a conception of the lyric which deterred him from that necessary accumulation of sense. He seems to have thought that the lyric required frailty: a flower quality: it must be as fresh, standing, and defined as a flower, and as frail. For the taste of our time, consequently, he could never solve, in a poem, the problem of scoring his music with sense rich enough to carry it. But in prose he could. It was a pertinent comment when he said that one leaf of "A Little Cloud" was worth more than *Chamber Music*.[11] He devoted nearly all his energy to prose because there he judged it right to impress a robust substance and score it densely, satisfyingly to the modern ear. Nevertheless, the music of the poems is worth seeking: a communication, however faint, of the voice of the world.

II

The better to see that the chamber *music* is what counts, I turn to a different aspect of the volume. Was it original? Joyce liked to appear before his city, his people, and his rivals as original: to upstage them with a display of easy intercourse with men of whom they had never heard but who were apparently Masters. But though the surprise performances of his youth came off, and though in his ultimate achievement he was so immensely original, he was not original at every moment of his progress. When, for example, he transposed Verlaine into Poem XXXV of *Chamber Music* he chose precisely the piece that most quickly made an appeal to the common English reader; Arthur Symons' translation of the same piece was to find its way into a popular anthology of world literature. In what might at this distance of sixty years seem to be the novelty of Joyce's affection for the lutesong, he was not novel. He was part of an English movement which has continued for another two generations, giving rise in literature to the sestinas and villanelles of the thirties, and in music to the revival of the sixteenth and seventeenth century composers and their forms and temper, and especially to the work of Benjamin Britten. He was not at the root of the movement. He was an offshoot from the main stem. The movement was a generation old when he published *Chamber Music*.

An essay by Francis Hueffer (father of Ford Madox Hueffer) is a useful signpost to the enquirer. In *Macmillan's Magazine*,

November, 1880, Hueffer wrote on "Troubadours, Ancient and Modern."[12] His modern troubadours were younger poets of the epoch, engaged in writing "rondeaux and roundels, villanelles and triolets." He named Arthur O'Shaughnessy, John Payne, E. W. Gosse, T. Marzials, Andrew Lang, Austin Dobson, and Mary Robinson, and quoted a triolet by Robert Bridges. During the two decades following his article, these troubadours were joined by others, including the Irishman whom Joyce regarded with some passion, Oscar Wilde.

So when Stephen, awaking towards dawn in a suffusion of music, experiences the word made flesh in the rhythmic recapitulations of the villanelle, he is not the first rediscoverer of the delight of this antique form. It is a glowing villanelle that he composes, shot with a romantic ardour. He fills the form with his own melody and movement. But in his choice of the form the innovator-to-be is not yet an innovator.

How another Irishman, who was as dexterous and virtuous with poetry as Joyce was to be with prose, could draw on the troubadour fashion and innovate with it, can be seen by a glance at three poems written by Yeats in three well-separated and markedly contrasting periods of his career. Among the perfect poems of *The Wind among the Reeds* is "He wishes for the Cloths of Heaven." There Yeats borrows from the modern troubadours by hinting, scarcely hinting, at their recurring phrases, and assimilates their method to his twilight style. Twenty years later he writes lines in which "I would be ignorant as the dawn" recurs as if in a rondeau, but grows to the surprise of "Ignorant and wanton as the dawn" (the rondeau is transformed by the Yeatsian dynamic). Twenty years later still, he writes the Crazy Jane sequence and the cognate ballads that depend on a refrain—thus assimilating the troubadour convention to the interclashing violence and tenderness of his final art. Feigning in his early days, when the troubadours were most the mode, to stand apart and to leave their exercises to his less profound friends among the rhymers, Yeats in fact stole their recapitulations and refrains, and stole with genius to add to his technical resources.

My impression of the relationship between Yeats and Joyce, while close to that proposed by W. Y. Tindall in his preface and notes to the Columbia University Press edition of *Chamber Music*,[13] differs a little from his, and particularly on a point of rhyme. The note to Poem XXVIII urges that Yeats inaugurated the technical experiments of his middle life, especially his experiments in distant and as I would say felicitous rhyme, or as Prof. Tindall says, "bad" rhyme, under the stimulus of *Chamber Music*. The argument is persuasively put, yet I am not quite persuaded. It is true that the rhymes of *Chamber Music* ring now and then like those of the later Yeats. In particular Joyce is successful, like Yeats, in rhyming monosyllable and plurisyllable. But there were already such rhymes in "To Ireland in the Coming Times." As for distant rhymes, the poet who had written "The Song of Wandering Aengus," in which an exquisite series of consonantal rhymes, "wood," "wand," "wing," threads the familiar vowel rhymes, did not need to learn the skill from Joyce. What he had to learn and did supremely learn from Joyce in due season was to face the real world: to face those "things uncomely and broken," by which he had been shocked in the nineties when they "wronged" his image of ideal beauty.[14] But he could not learn that from *Chamber Music,* whose troubadour, another idealizer as troubadours are, had still to teach himself the lesson.

For the technique of lyric, Joyce was entirely willing to go to school with Yeats. He marvellously renders homage to Yeats the technician in the passage of *A Portrait* which recalls the playing of *The Countess Cathleen* in Dublin, the jeering incomprehension of Stephen's fellow students, and Stephen's enchantment.[15] "A soft liquid joy flowed through the words where the soft long vowels hurtled noiselessly and fell away, lapping and flowing back and ever shaking the white bells of their waves in mute chime and mute peal and soft low swooning cry": — that is his experience of Yeats' dramatic verse. The metrical modulations of *Chamber Music* must at least have been encouraged by the iamb-qualifying metrics of *The Wind among the Reeds* and Aleel's songs in *The Countess Cathleen*. What is striking, perhaps, is that Joyce could incorporate the metrical lessons of Yeats without any of the more obvious signs of imitation. He liked to dissemble his debts to his immediate elders, at least if they shared the same language. Although the lyrics of *Chamber Music* are modern troubadour songs, they avoid a too evident association with the movement: there is not a roundel or villanelle among them; yet to the eye of the historian certain usages (the prohibition "O bend no more," and the exploitation of the adaptable noun "ways") clearly connect them with the villanelle of *A Portrait*. Joyce prefers the Shakespearean or Jonsonian song to differentiate himself from the Dobsons; and to imply, perhaps, that refrains are obstacles for schoolboys, relatively easy for a poet to leap, and that he will do the harder thing, meet the demands of an archaic form "free and living." By the same step he differentiates himself from Yeats. When Yeats heard some of the early Joyce poems in the autumn of 1902 he was amazed at their technique: ". . . much better than the technique of any young Dublin man I have met during my time. It might have been the work of a young man who had lived in an Oxford literary set."[16] That last sentence is not ironic. It means that he saw the poems as an exacting development of the modern troubadouring of England. It also means that the form had beguiled him into overlooking his own influence, which he would have recognized in Irish forms or themes or in the smoke of theosophical imagery.

III

But of course the form was not chosen for the sake of concealment. That was an incidental benefit. It was chosen because it belonged to a Weltanschauung, a stance, a "style" of life. In plotting the relative unoriginality of the "modern troubadour" form, I have no intention of depreciating its value or the function or the value of the Joycean stance. The archaic lyricist was an essential part of Joyce and his work.

An essential half. There were two Joyces: the lyrical and the satirical; the singer and the clown. At the beginning of his writing life they were well-split halves: he was the complete schizophrene. The personality ascendant in *Chamber Music* was the courtier, the punctualist, the grave and dainty singer. The other personality was the obscenist, the ribald rapscallion, the brayer. In Joyce's outward daily behaviour at twenty-two the latter seems to have been better-known to the Dubliners (though Stanislaus tells of his craving for good manners even then).[17] As he grew older the courtier became the conductor of his living; he would let no one outvie him in etiquette. The movement in his works was towards the ascendancy of the rollicker. But not, I hasten to add, to the exclusion of the lyricist. That is the subject of my story.

Thanks to Richard Ellmann's scholarship, we have a document which tells us a great deal about both personalities and their goings-on and gettings-together. It is the *Giacomo Joyce* notebook of the last prewar period in Trieste. At once lachrymose and animated, it helps to explain the lifelong survival of the Courtier in Joyce, and accordingly his role in *Chamber Music*.

We may sometimes ask ourselves why so stern a literary critic as Joyce permitted himself his luteplaying, and the idealizing daintiness to which Ellmann, nearly as stern, has attached the damning label "prettified."[18] *Giacomo Joyce* shows that the literary critic knew the limitations of the style but also discerned a value at its core:

> Jan Pieters Sweelink. The quaint name of the old Dutch musician makes all beauty seem quaint and far. I hear his variations for the clavichord on an old air: *Youth has an end*. In the vague mist of old sounds a faint point of light appears: the speech of the soul is about to be heard.[19]

The limitations are the distance and faintness of the revelation. The justification is, that the revelation comes: "the speech of the soul."

Written some ten years after the *Chamber Music* songs, *Giacomo Joyce* makes use more explicitly than they of an old-world setting and old-world locutions. Joyce transposes Amalia Popper's home across five centuries: "Wintry air in the castle, gibbeted coats of mail . . . " A servant interrupts the lesson with the announcement of a visitor: "There is one below would speak with your ladyship." On a later occasion Joyce seeks (but in the safe realm of interior dialogue) a rapport with Amalia, and when she apparently trembles before his adult approach he reassures her in a lutanist's phrase: "Nay, be not afraid." Later still he fancies that he has possessed her in a wordless, touchless interpenetration of looks, and accepts that as the most consummate of all possible conquests and resigns the physical Amalia to any lucky later-comer: "Take her now who will!" Listen to these phrases with not a troubadour's but a theatre-goer's sensibility, and you may contend that they are lifted from the dialogue of Victorian melodrama. There was certainly the oddest communication in the Joycean memory-chambers between the refined-and-archaic and the Victorian-and-plush. But it is evident from his castle scenery that he himself dated his language and stance as antique. That "elegant and antique phrase," which he had made as if to abjure in Poem XXVII of *Chamber Music*, alleging that he knew that the reality of love was different from the troubadour's ideal, he still uttered. It was irrepressible and indispensable.

However, the lyric gentleman who was the soliloquist of *Chamber Music* no longer has matters all to himself in 1913. The Other Joyce interrupts, halloos, heckles, and more and more asserts his counterstrain. Lyric twists into comedy. "Love me, love my umbrella." The two personae compete for the stage. If the graver affects to be alone, the Other cavorts around him and pokes him with bum and truncheon. This is a decisive development. The notebook drives a road towards *Ulysses*.

In *Ulysses* Joyce makes a masterpiece out of the cooperation of his two selves. As the current lore of our mid-twentieth-century tells, the schizophrene who elevates his conflict into art does it not by slaying either of the partners but by bringing them into a relationship where both live and fulfill themselves in a totality that is greater than their sum. The multifarious power of *Ulysses* arises from the integration of the Two Joyces, the coordination of what they both know and their different ways of saying it. The ribald comedian gets his heroic fling, and the lyricist still discourses in a flow of music. The vision opens, clearer, nearer. Tributes have been paid, as they must be, to the comedian as the vision-bidder. Our concern here is with Orpheus and his lute as visionary and instrument of the vision. Of course, the music of the epic is often rich beyond the dainty range of *Chamber Music:* "Yes, bronze from anear, by gold from afar, heard steel from anear, hoofs ring from afar . . ."[20] But when Joyce wishes most precisely to elicit "the speech of the soul," he still uses the simplest lyrical phrase. So as he approaches the culmination of Molly's monologue: "he said I was a flower of the mountain."[21] If we turn to that and look at it in a ruthless mood, we may feel not unfamiliar qualms about the suspension of Joyce's literary censorship. Has he relaxed the control when he should have exerted it sternly? He does not think so. He is working at full stretch here, and if he employs the lyrical method it is because he believes in it. He expects us not to turn and look at the phrase, but to come to it on the tide of continuous reading: to understand the style by going all the way with him through the vicissitudes in which it inheres; and thus to feel it and hear it as he does.

An event in the history of *Chamber Music* connects alike with the occurrence of that lyric phrase at the climax of *Ulysses* and with the whole problem of Joyce's valuation of his lyrical self. During the crisis of 1909 when Joyce fell victim to Cosgrave's slander of Nora and wrote to her in agonized abuse, then feared that he had destroyed his contact with her and that he would never repossess the pleasure and nourishment of her tenderness unless he could undo his outburst, one of his gestures of propitiation was to quote *Chamber Music* to her.[22] And she, astonishingly, took up the volume and read it. He did not pretend that he had written the poems for her. On the contrary he admitted that they were conceived for an imaginary ceremonious lady of a tower: "a girl fashioned into a curious grave beauty by the culture of generations before her." By contrast Nora was, as we can see at this distance, Reality, earthy and sound, a physical wife, a healing force. Yet the poems *were* for Nora, he went on to say, because there was "something in you higher than anything I had put into them." Joyce was sure, and remained sure long after his love had "waxed all too wise," that in Real Woman there springs the point of light or the point of life or a flower, and that Real Woman longs for its recognition and for a man's worship of it. Molly, after she has had her romp with the large Blazes Boylan, still cares for Bloom because he feels for her and for all women with this lyric intuition:

> ... yes so we are flowers all a womans body yes that was one true thing he said in his life and the sun shines for you today yes that was why I liked him because I saw he understood or felt what a woman is ...

In 1909 it helped Joyce to expunge his mistake and win Nora back when the poems of *Chamber Music* reminded his wife that he "understood or felt what a woman is." They reminded her not by saying it, but singing it.

The episode may have confirmed to Joyce that the *Chamber Music* poems secrete the light of reality at the core of their idealism, and that song is the most compelling testimony of life, that the lyrical method must never be dropped. It might be enriched, but not dropped.

Wherever Joyce strove, and he strove persistently, to broach the light of reality, he relied on music. We can never go towards that point of light. It will recede if we press forward. It can only grow towards us, and will only come if beckoned, conjured—and can best be conjured by music. Joyce had been impressed, say Mason and Ellmann in their notes to *The Critical Writings*,[23] by the last line in Verlaine's "Art Poétique": *"Et tout le reste est littérature."* It may be so; but he was more impressed by the first line: *"De la musique avant toute chose."* It was his own innate conviction, his own innate practice. We are always impressed to find that we are right to do what we do.

IV

"The speech of the soul" formed in the vague mist of antique music, but the flower of *Ulysses* was Molly's body, not her soul. As the singer and the obscenist coalesced and Joyce's art strengthened, the speech of the soul became the song of the earth. In the last opus, *Finnegans Wake,* the world speaks: its rivers, its thunder. Since the effects of a major book spread in ripples through the ensuing decades, it has naturally followed that the better entertainment of our present time listens for the music of the world. An instance is the scene in Fellini's *La Dolce Vita* in which the tape-recorder, in the elegant room in Rome, plays back the menacing eddies of the cosmic winds.

To revisit *Chamber Music* with that outcome of the opera in mind is to seek the first tape of the speech of the soul which is also the first tape of the world-voice. Joyce recorded it in Poem XXXIV. As he told Geoffrey Molyneux Palmer, the composer who set the songs, Poem XXXIV is dramatically the last of the sequence (XXXV and XXXVI are tailpieces).[24] Two forces are registered: the winter that menaces outside the door and forbids rest; the breathing of the sleep of a heart soothed by a poet's gentleness. The melancholy of the cosmic winter drifts through the music, but there is a lulling countermotion, a berceuse, the warmth, the protection of the pleasure of art; and the music involves, however faintly felt, faintly heard, an equilibrium of the two forces, the two rhythms. There are four vocative "O"s in this short poem. They are unnecessary to the meaning, almost unnecessary to the metre, for the poem would be metrically sufficient without them; but they are right for the music. A composer, and a singer, would make something of them. When the music comes to life in us in the days after the reading, they play their part.

The music of Poem XXXIV, faint but haunting, grows into the winter rhapsody of the last paragraph of "The Dead," with which Joyce begins to realize his orchestral powers. Then the maturation of a quarter of a century goes forward. In *Chamber Music* the paucity of the success, it has been suggested, lies in the paucity of the sense. In the subsequent books the sense gains in body. It engages the intellect in its own right in *Dubliners* and *A Portrait,* perhaps occasionally over-engages it to the neglect of the musical flow. In *Ulysses* there is the most satisfying interplay of sense and sound. But in certain sections of *Ulysses,* and in the whole of *Finnegans Wake* to which they look forward, a curious thing happens. "The sense must be the medium of the sound"; but Joyce plaits layer on layer of sense; and that almost defeats his purpose; not perhaps by his fault, but by our habits, which, however, he might have forseen. We are readers of literature, not listeners to music. We are much, much worse than our ancestors, of whom Ben Jonson bitterly complained that they were beginning to use their eyes and stop their ears. We are eye-folk on the verge of deafness. The glaucomatic Joyce was not. With Shakespeare, Jonson, and Milton he was all inclining ear. We go to work with our eyes on *Finnegans Wake,* as the spelling tempts us to, laboring to analyze the layers of sense into their components. It is salutary to turn repeatedly to the letter in which Joyce tells Miss Weaver that he is "considerably wound up" after proofreading *Anna Livia Plurabelle,* that the "sing-song" fills his addled head, and that till it fades he cannot deal with the news of the day.[25] To be filled with the singsong must be the hope of every devotee of *Finnegans Wake.* We are brought to the right condition whenever we listen to an Irishman reading the work, or anyone reading it with the resources of the tenor voice. These aids failing, we must read it aloud ourselves. Even if we are non-Celts and even if we are crows, the sound will be better than anything the eye alone can afford. Yet though I say this as essential doctrine, I must not make it exclusive doctrine. Since Joyce took the risk of plying his sense closely, he obviously wanted the crisscross to play a part in the total effect; and it is doubtful whether the ear can pick up half the ambiguities that are within the comprehension of the eye. It may be that Joyce overtaxed the capacity of every reader with so intricate a polyphony of sense and sound. I leave that topic to my wiser colleagues. Assuming *ad interim* what we like to assume of a master, that he is always right, let us justify him by saying that in *Finnegans Wake* the musical love of God and the intellectual love of God and the bodily love of God meet and merge.

    One last consideration. Joyce presented himself in *Chamber Music* as a neoclassicist and as a perfectionist who shaped faultless lyrics and assembled them in an impeccable book. Yet the last lyric is ill-chosen if a book of perfect proportions is the objective, and ill-chosen if the objective of the book is consonance.

Poem XXXVI has been praised to the neglect of the preceding thirty-five. It *is* a good poem. But it is not archaic, and it is not chamber music. It works in a style with which Yeats had experimented in "Do you not hear me calling" and "I hear the white horses," a style far from softness or daintiness, a style that bids for the furious energy of the horses of passion, a style that, regardless of all daedalian animadversions on the Celtic Revival, draws on the imagery of the Red Branch and the battle-cars. How are we to account for its presence after Poem XXXIV and that perfect winter ending? We may contrive this reason: that Poems XXXV and XXXVI go on to register sharply the hostility of the winter, of the outer elements, within which Joyce had quietened his love to her long sleep. More, it registers the terror within the beauty, that violence in the cosmos, which lady and poet who lean their ear for the lovely sounds of the world will catch in the undersong—catch and lose and never cease to lean for till they have caught it again and notated what the sea murmurs and the thunder says. By this argument we may claim that the final poems issue organically from the volume, though as a disproportionate and fearsome cauda or coda. But we must add another reason. Joyce and his brother, who helped him to arrange the volume, subordinated their sense of perfection to a romantic passion from which neither they nor some of their foremost neoclassical coevals, including T. S. Eliot, were free: the love of the grand curtain. George Moore was, for better or worse, more genuinely neoclassical: he deliberately cultivated the "minor" ending, the dying fall. In this matter Joyce was romantic and Wagnerian. *Dubliners* culminates in "The Dead," extensive beyond any of the preceding stories, resonant beyond any of them, its own end soaring away from Dublin. *A Portrait* is *formally* neoclassical, touched with the sense of the downbeat ending as the narrative cracks into fragments of diary, utterly right to convey approaching departure and the disconnecting of the son, tissue by tissue, from the body of home; but *emotionally* it is romantic, fervidly charged with the ritual of self-dedication and intimations of immortality. *Ulysses* is the most famous example in literature of the concentration of every power in the final chapter and the unremitting amplification of the power through the last page and the last word. The final page of *Finnegans Wake* is correspondingly intense, cosmic, Wagnerian. But here, for his last bow, Joyce pulls one new trick from his reserves and exhilaratingly synthesizes his romantic and neoclassical modes: the purple curtain, seeming to descend on a *Liebestod,* suddenly furls back again, and by a dream-transformation everything is where it was at the start, and death is birth and there is no end but resumption. The final page of *Finnegans Wake* does on the largest scale what the lyrics of *Chamber Music* do in miniature, loops back to the first line. A nice example of the consistency and unity of Joyce's art. But such examples are many; this anniversary book may well be full of them.

3

THE JOYCE
OF *DUBLINERS*

James S. Atherton

When *Dubliners* first appeared, on June 15, 1914, it attracted little attention. The stories generally described as "a little pointless" or "trivial," although Gerald Gould in the London *New Statesman* believed he had recognized the emergence of a genius already developed and fixed in a somewhat morbid mould, and an anonymous reviewer in the Liverpool *Daily Courier* (a paper which gave particular attention to Irish affairs) admired the power of the "sunless, searching and relentless stories."[1] Only Ezra Pound, writing in *The Egoist*, which had been publishing *A Portrait* in installments since February 2, 1914, gave Joyce's stories unqualified, if somewhat negative, praise. Pound began by welcoming the "freedom from sloppiness" of Joyce's "clear hard prose," and went on to say that "Araby," for instance, is much better than a "story," it is a "vivid waiting." Still more percipiently he wrote: "He gives us Dublin as it presumably is . . . . He gives us things as they are, not only for Dublin, but for every city . . . . That is to say, the author is quite capable of dealing with things about him, and dealing directly, yet these details do not engross him, he is capable of getting at the universal element beneath them."[2] Pound went on to praise Joyce for his "rigorous selection of detail," and claimed for him "a very definite place among contemporary English prose writers."

But, even allowing for the cool reception given by most critics, and the lack of interest in new writing that followed the outbreak of war, it is surprising that the book sold so slowly, for its prepublication history might have been expected to gain for it at least a *succès de scandale*. Full accounts of the difficulties which Joyce encountered may be read in Richard Ellmann's *James Joyce*,[3] and several other works.[4] The story is long and involved, and I shall merely outline it here.

Grant Richards, a London publisher, accepted the book with its original twelve stories on February 17, 1906, but wrote on April 23rd that his printer had marked some "objectionable passages" in the story "Two Gallants" which Joyce had meanwhile added. Joyce wrote, asking indignantly why the printer was "allowed to open his mouth," but Richards stood by his printer—probably because he could not afford the expense of a possible law suit. The passages objected to seem quite acceptable today: the occasional use of the word "bloody," references to "a man with two establishments to keep up," and a woman who "continued to cast bold glances . . . and changed the position of her legs often"; but, although Joyce made several concessions, such as deleting the word "bloody" in six places, the printer was not appeased. When Joyce unwisely asked why, if the story "Counterparts" was objected to, there was no objection to "An Encounter," Richards, whose suspicions had been aroused, replied by objecting to "An Encounter," and in September rejected the book altogether. It was then rejected by several other publishers, and even by the literary agent recommended by Arthur Symons.[5]

In April, 1909, the Dublin publishers, Maunsel and Company, accepted the book and had actually printed it before a fresh set of objections so frightened them that they destroyed all the copies. This time it was for fear of libel actions, and, although Joyce never recognized it, this fear was justifiable. An English barrister-at-law, whom I consulted over this point, gave his opinion that Maunsel and Company would have been liable to conviction of libel if they had published *Dubliners* in Dublin in 1910. He added that once a publisher's attention had been drawn to the libellous nature of any material, whether by his printer or any member of the public, then no defense could have justified the publication of the material. Writers nowadays often protect themselves by declaring that all their characters are imaginary. Joyce admitted that his characters were often based on real people, and most of the places they went to had an actual existence in Dublin, so the possibility of litigation was very real. What arouses one's sympathy for Joyce, however, is that Maunsel and Company took over a year to realize this danger. Joyce decided that the year had been employed by his enemies in attacking his work by secret methods. He wrote *Gas from a Burner* to relieve his feelings and sent *Dubliners* to some more publishers. Then, on November 25, 1913, Grant Richards asked to see the book again and agreed to publish it. His printer this time had no moral scruples, and probably did not know that it presented real people in actual places.

The long delay had one good result: there were now fifteen stories, the final one being "The Dead," Joyce's masterpiece in this genre. Most of the recent critical attention paid to *Dubliners* by nonspecialists has concentrated on this story, which will be considered later in this chapter. However, it seems natural to discuss the earlier stories first, and also at this point it would be well, perhaps, to reflect on Joyce's method of composition.

Before he began writing the stories of *Dubliners,* Joyce had tried various literary forms. The most interesting of these, from its effect on his later work, was a series of what he called "Epiphanies." The nature of these is described most clearly in *Stephen Hero,* where we are told that "By an epiphany he meant a sudden spiritual manifestation, whether in the vulgarity of speech or of gesture or of a memorable phase of the mind itself."[6] Every Catholic child is taught to use the word for the Feast on January 6 which celebrates the revelation of God, in the person of the child Jesus, to the three Magi who represented the gentiles. No doubt Joyce met the word again in the *Etymological Dictionary* by Skeat, which he says in *Stephen Hero,* Stephen Daedalus "read . . . by the hour,"[7] and which defines the word as "manifestation, showing forth." It has become one of Joyce's major contributions to the vocabulary of literary criticism as a term for the sudden realization of a thing in all its full and unique significance. In practice Joyce's epiphanies usually showed the reality to be less attractive and praiseworthy than might have been expected. Samuel Butler used the word in the same sense in the "Higgledy-Piggledy" section of his *Notebooks* when he imagined himself seeing "Providence," and wrote a passage entitled "Epiphany," which reads:

> If Providence could be seen at all, he would probably turn out to be a very disappointing person—a little wizened old gentleman with a cold in his head, a red nose and a comforter round his neck, whistling o'er the furrow'd land or crooning to himself as he goes aimlessly along the streets, poking his way about and loitering continually at shopwindows and second-hand bookstalls.

On the other hand, Joyce's epiphany could be that "explosion out of darkness" which Gerard Manley Hopkins described—a kind of mystical experience when a part of the veil shrouding the mystery of the world was suddenly drawn aside so that the true nature of things seemed revealed. A chapter in W. T. Noon's *Joyce and Aquinas,* entitled "How Culious an Epiphany," deals with Joyce's epiphanies from this standpoint, and gives references to the numerous critical articles which have been devoted to this aspect of Joyce's aesthetic theorizing.[8]

Joyce was composing his epiphanies at the same time as he was writing the long quasi-biographical novel part of which has survived as *Stephen Hero,* and some of the verses which he published later as *Chamber Music.* However, he told Yeats in 1902 that he had "thrown over metrical form that he might get a form so fluent that it would respond to the motions of the spirit." He must have shown some of his epiphanies to Yeats at this time, for Yeats wrote of Joyce's "beautiful though immature and eccentric harmony of little prose descriptions and meditations."[9] Joyce seems to have been searching in various directions for a topic and a technique on which to employ the genius for writing which he was sure he possessed, and at the same time to have been trying to impress all the literary figures he could meet with the importance of that genius.

One of the main literary figures in Dublin at the time was George Russell, who had gained a reputation as a poet on the strength of some verse that now seems rather sapless, published under the pen name A.E., and who was a leader in various enterprises such as the Irish Agricultural Association. A kindly man, he was known as a patron of young writers and in 1903 published *New Songs, A Lyric Selection,* which was an anthology of verse by Padraic Colum and other young Irish writers whom Russell thought promising. Joyce was not asked to contribute to this book, but he cultivated Russell's acquaintance and showed him some chapters of *Stephen Hero.* Russell liked the novel and asked Joyce to write some stories for a magazine called *Irish Homestead.* What he wanted, he said, was "a piece of simple, rural, live-making, pathos," and he told Joyce that the pound a story he offered could be easily earned if Joyce "did not mind playing to the common understanding and liking for once in a way."[10]

It is easy to understand the dilemma in which this kindly request placed Joyce. He wanted recognition as a writer and needed money, but he wished to become known as a writer of a kind diametrically opposite to those whose work appeared in *Irish Homestead*—a weekly for farmers. The first version of the story "The Sisters," which appeared in *Irish Homestead* on August 13, 1904, shows his original indecision about his attitude. This original version is reprinted in full in Magalaner's *Time of Apprenticeship, the Fiction of Young James Joyce*.[11] Much shorter than the final version, it begins:

> Three nights in succession I had found myself in Great Britain-street at that hour, as if by Providence. Three nights also I had raised my eyes to that lighted square of window and speculated. I seemed to understand that it would occur at night. But in spite of the Providence that had led my feet, and in spite of the reverent curiosity of my eyes, I had discovered nothing. Each night the square was lighted in the same way, faintly and evenly. It was not the light of candles, so far as I could see. Therefore, it had not yet occurred.
>
> On the fourth night at that hour I was in another part of the city. It may have been the same Providence that led me there—a whimsical kind of Providence to take me at a disadvantage. As I went home I wondered was that square of window lighted as before, or did it reveal the ceremonious candles in whose light the Christian must take his last sleep. I was not surprised, then, when at supper I found myself a prophet. Old Cotter and my uncle were talking at the fire, smoking. Old Cotter is the old distiller who owns the batch of prize setters. He used to be very interesting when I knew him first, talking about "faints" and "worms." Now I find him tedious.

A comparison of this with the beginning of the story as it was finally published will make clear the point I am stressing: Joyce was not sure what he was trying to do in the first version. He wanted to please his rural Catholic readers, and their editor, and yet he wanted to shock and puzzle them. His divided intentions result in a piece of very undistinguished prose, but it is hardly fair to criticize Joyce for the defects in the first version of a story which he revised so competently. One feature in it, however, seems worth comment since it illustrates a Joycean trait which he retained all his life—a fondness for playing tricks on his readers. Presumably Joyce hopes that some dog-fancying farmers would be confused as to whether the "faints" and "worms" were disorders of Old Cotter's setters, or the weak spirits produced at the start and finish of the distilling process and the tube that is used for distilling. In the final version, however, the dogs are omitted. And the mention of Great Britain-street, which strikes a false note, is removed to a less conspicuous position. In general the first version lacks focus. The final one begins with the precise note that Joyce intends: hopelessness, paralysis. In place of the uneasy "ceremonious candles" we have the simple and effective, "I knew that two candles must be set at the head of a corpse." The character of the narrator, which is not in evidence in the first version, appears almost at once. He is a child fascinated by words and both attracted and repelled by the evil which he sees around him.

One other feature of the first version, which owed nothing to Joyce, may be mentioned here. It is the name given to the church at which the priest, whose death the story tells, had served. In *Irish Homestead* it is St. Ita's—a nonexistent church. Joyce had written "S. Catherine's, Meath Street" but the editor altered this to avoid annoying anyone. When the book was printed Joyce once again used the name of the real church. It was the accumulation of such details which was responsible for his troubles with Maunsel and Company.

By the time Joyce had finished the first version of "The Sisters," he had solved the problem of his attitude: there was to be no lowering of his standards to please the common taste. In an undated letter to C. P. Curran he wrote, "I am writing a series of epicleti—ten—for a paper. I have written one. I call the series *Dubliners* to betray the soul of that hemiplegia or paralysis which many consider a city."[12] The word "epicleti" is explained by Richard Ellmann as referring to an invocation in the Greek ritual in which "the Holy Ghost is besought to transform the host into the body and blood of Christ."[13] Ellmann goes on, very convincingly, to quote as a further explanation a passage from Stanislaus Joyce's *My Brother's Keeper:* "Don't you think, said he [Joyce] reflectively, choosing his words without haste, there is a certain resemblance between the mystery of the Mass and what I am trying to do? I mean that I am trying in my poems to give people some kind of intellectual pleasure or spiritual enjoyment by converting the bread of everyday life into something that has a permanent artistic life of its own."[14] The discussion with Stanislaus was about religion, and the mention of poems makes it unlikely that *Dubliners* was in Joyce's mind, but the use of the word "epicleti" in the letter to Curran shows conclusively that Joyce did sometimes think of his stories as epiphanies, "converting the bread of everyday life into something that has a permanent artistic life of its own."

At first he had no doubt as to the nature of the reality of the "everyday life" of Dublin which his epiphanies were to present and preserve. In a letter to Grant Richards he wrote, "the expression 'Dubliner' seems to me to bear some meaning and I doubt whether the same can be said for such words as 'Londoner' or 'Parisian,' both of which have been used by authors as titles . . . so that I think people might be willing to pay for the special odour of corruption which, I hope, floats over my stories."[15] This "special odour" is apparent from the opening paragraph of the first story with its carefully chosen words—*no hope, if he was dead, the head of a corpse, paralysis, simony, fear* . . . . And the effect is achieved in all the early stories. We are told of a corpse which, when alive, wore clothes with "a green faded look," and had "discoloured teeth." The boys in "An Encounter" wandered "through squalid streets" and met with a man "shabbily dressed in a suit of greenish-black" and with "yellow teeth." The boy in "Araby" runs past "the back doors of the dark dripping gardens where odours arose from the ashpits," and Eveline, in the story of that name, is twice described as inhaling "the odour of dusty cretonne." Dublin is "a channel of poverty and inaction" in the first paragraph of

"After the Race," and never attains a higher attribution than "the mask of a capital." Unpleasant and brutal fathers dominate the majority of homes.

Stanislaus Joyce wrote that his brother had determined, even when he was at school, to expose the sordidness of domestic life in Dublin, which they both believed was being concealed by the various married women whom they knew.[16] Later in his book Stanislaus gives the outline of a story, *Silhouettes,* written by his brother when at school.[17] The narrator is watching the shadows on a window blind and sees "the burly figure of a man, staggering and threatening with upraised fist, and the smaller sharp-faced figure of a nagging woman. A blow is struck and the light goes out. The narrator waits to see if anything happens afterwards. Yes, the window-blind is illuminated again dimly, by a candle no doubt, and the woman's sharp profile appears again accompanied by two small heads, just above the window-ledge, of children wakened by the noise. The woman's finger is pointed in warning. She is saying, 'Don't wake Pa.' " Stanislaus is using the outline to prove two things: that life in Dublin was unpleasant, and that his brother shared this view wholeheartedly as he exploited "the minute unpromising details of his immediate experience."[18] Neither of these conclusions is acceptable. Unlike his brother, who remained inflexibly at enmity with his father and everything that could be considered typically Irish, James Joyce was at once attracted and repelled. The first paragraph of *Dubliners,* which Joyce used, as he later used the first paragraphs of *Finnegans Wake,* to state the themes with which the rest of the work would be concerned, ends with a sentence that expresses his original attitude: "It filled me with fear, and yet I longed to be nearer to it and to look upon its deadly work." But as he grew older, and as he lived in other countries, he began to appreciate some of the virtues of the Irish and their way of life. Richard Ellmann says that it was the effect of southern Europe on Joyce that caused his anger to cool and his aim to shift "imperceptibly from exposure to revelation of his countrymen,"[19] and certainly it was not until he had lived for some time in southern Europe that Joyce remembered that he had omitted to portray the hospitality of the Irish. He wrote to Stanislaus from Rome, which he was finding inhospitable, "I have not reproduced its [Ireland's] ingenuous insularity and its hospitality, the latter 'virtue' so far as I can see does not exist elsewhere in Europe."[20] Joyce's attitude is, as usual, far from simple. He may, as Ellmann says, have mellowed as Ibsen did in the warm Mediterranean atmosphere; he also found that the inhabitants of other cities could be even more unpleasant than those of his own.

But there was one opinion about Dublin which Joyce never altered. He makes Mr. Doran in "The Boarding House" reflect that "Dublin is such a small city: everyone knows everyone else's business." In *Finnegans Wake* there is an entire paragraph embroidering upon this idea: "Retire to rest before misturbing your nighboor, mankind of baffling descriptions. Others are as tired of themselves as you are . . . .[21] Every ditcher's dastard in Dupling will let us know about it if you have paid the mulctman by whether your rent is open to be foreclosed or aback in your arrears. This is seriously meant. Here is a homelet not a hothel."[22] Amongst other things this is telling us that Dublin is a small town—a hamlet, a little home, the inhabitants of which know all about each other's business. And Joyce himself seems to have shared the native Dublin interest in other people's affairs, and takes most of his plots either from his own family's experiences or from what he heard about others. This, of course, is quite usual with writers. Turgenev, for example, said that he always wrote about his own experience. But it must be remembered that much of the evidence for the sources of the stories in *Dubliners* comes from the writings of

Stanislaus Joyce, who does not seem to be a completely reliable witness, and who often overemphasizes his own part in his brother's work.

The publication of Stanislaus' *Dublin Diary* has revealed several instances of his having altered to his own advantage the account of events related differently in his earlier published, but much later written, *My Brother's Keeper*. For example, Stanislaus remarks, after he has been unjustly accused of borrowing a witticism, which, in fact his brother had borrowed from him, that "Cosgrave . . . obviously thought I was found out, properly caught in the act. But as Jim said nothing, neither did I."[23] In his *Dublin Diary* he wrote, "I suppose Cosgrave thought that here was evident proof. I was foolish enough to tell him that I had made the remark to Jim a year ago, and Jim admitted it. The best revenge I could have taken would have been to let Cosgrave feel happy in the sense of having convicted me."[24] This sort of manipulation of events to satisfy one's self-esteem is forgivable enough, but, although it softens our opinion of the intransigent Stanislaus, it must lower his value as a reliable witness. And, so far as the stories in *Dubliners* are concerned, Stanislaus' evidence would go to show that many of the characters and events are based on his experience rather than his brother's. It seems to me much more likely that Joyce used his own experience, and that Stanislaus exaggerates the occasional borrowings which his brother made.

It is, however, from Stanislaus Joyce that we can trace the original events on which some of Joyce's stories are based, and, as Richard Ellmann has said, Joyce "frequently borrowed initial hints for his stories from Stanislaus: for 'The Dead,' Stanislaus's description of an Irish tenor's way of singing a sepulchral chorus in a song of Tom Moore; for 'A Painful Case,' Stanislaus's account of a meeting with a married woman at a concert."[25] The priest of "The Sisters" is based on a real clergyman who was related to Joyce's mother. Stanislaus denied this, stating that, "In the preface to the American edition of *Dubliners*,[26] Padraic Colum says that this story ['Araby'] and 'The Sisters' are evidently recollections of childhood. This is a mistake. In fact only two of the stories—'An Encounter' and 'A Mother,' describing a concert at which my brother sang with John McCormack—are based on his actual personal experience. The remaining stories are either pure fiction or elaborated at second hand from the experiences of others, mostly from mine, as I shall show later."[27] But the bazaar which the small boy in "Araby" visited actually took place. Ellmann's *James Joyce* includes a reproduction of the "Official Catalogue" for it, dated May 14th to 19th, 1894,[28] and the conversation recorded as overheard from the "young lady who was talking and laughing with two young gentlemen" had first been noted by Joyce as an "Epiphany." And, if I may quote again from Ellman's biography, to which all Joyceans must be constantly indebted: "William and John [Murray—Joyce's uncles] are the two brothers, Joe and Alphy, sketched in the story 'Clay' in *Dubliners,* who are not on speaking terms with each other. Maria, the little laundress who tries to make peace between them, was also a relative of the Murrays, and one of whom May Joyce was especially fond. On the Flynn side of the family was the priest described in 'The Sisters,' who became harmlessly insane and lost his parish. . . . It was William's child who said at the end of 'Counterparts,' 'I'll say a Hail Mary for you, pa, if you don't beat me,' but with artistic dispassionateness that transcended family quarrels, Farrington's impudent, frustrated character in that story fuses William Murray's temperament with John Joyce's."[29]

From the biographical aspect, as from all others, the most interesting of the stories is "The Dead." Here again we are indebted to Professor Ellmann for establishing the facts. Chapter XV of his *James Joyce* is entitled "The Backgrounds of The Dead." In this chapter Ellmann shows how Joyce carefully selected details from his own life and used real characters and events to build up his story. He even made use of sentences from his own love letters: "Why is it that words like these seem to me so dull and cold? Is it because there is no word tender enough to be your name?"[30] And the basic situation, of the man who finds that his wife is still remembering with affection a boy who loved her and is now dead, is one which Joyce found himself in. Nora Joyce's boy lover had been called Sonny Bodkin. Joyce went to the extent of visiting his grave in the remote country churchyard and saw "the crooked crosses and headstones . . . the spears of the little gate." The central character, Gabriel Conroy, is a blending of James Joyce, and, as Stanislaus tells us, his father, whose annual duty it was to carve and make a speech at the Misses Flynn's dinner. This creation of a work of art out of his memories is typical of all Joyce's work.

With the choice of name for his story's hero we come to another typical feature, the hidden acknowledgement of a literary source, for Joyce took the name from the hero of a novel by Bret Harte. Why, it may be asked, should a writer bother to take a name from another writer's work? It would seem that the invention of a name requires very little creative talent. But in fact Joyce also borrowed from Harte's novel something much more subtle and useful to him as a writer. Harte begins his story with a rhythmical description of the snow that covers the Sierras: "Snow. Everywhere . . . . It had been snowing for ten days; snowing in finely granulated powder, in damp spongy flakes, in thin feathery plumes, snowing from a leaden sky steadily, snowing fiercely . . ." This rhythm from Harte's *Gabriel Conroy* provided exactly what Joyce wanted for the end of "The Dead." The borrowing was first pointed out by Gerhard Friedrich[31] who suggests that Joyce also based his heroine's name, Gretta, on the name of Harte's heroine, Grace, for the first name is a variant of the second. This may or may not be so, but I have no doubt that Joyce's use of the name Gabriel Conroy for his hero is meant as an acknowledgment of his borrowing of the rhythm. This device of hidden acknowledgments was frequently used in *Finnegans Wake,* but it is in this story that he employed it for the first time. Another source from which Joyce borrowed, George Moore's *Vain Fortune,* was first noticed by Professor Ellmann.[32] What Joyce took from this book was the series of events which ends his story: the inability of lovers to come together because of a memory of a dead lover which comes between them. Joyce gives no clue to this borrowing, or to any others in *Dubliners,* except that from Bret Harte.

A great deal has been written on the literary models Joyce used for the tone, attitude, method, and so on, of his stories. He has been compared with Chekhov and Maupassant. He has been described as a realist following Flaubert and Zola,[33] cutting out his slices of life with precision. He has been written about exhaustively as a symbolist until there is scarcely a factual detail in his stories which some critic has not found symbolic.[34] And although this symbol-seeking has been overemphasized, it has added something worthwhile to our understanding of Joyce's work. But Joyce was not merely a symbolist. His aim was always to avoid following the ideas of any group and to work out his own way of writing.

His stories owe much of their strength and interest to the variety of techniques employed on them. We have seen that, in spite of Stanislaus' claims, Joyce nearly always began with an incident from his own experience. This factual basis was a necessity to him and he believed that there was no other way of writing. He once said he "suspected that Ibsen met the four or five characters that he uses for all his plays before he was twenty-five."[35] Shakespeare, according to Stephen Dedalus in *Ulysses,* "drew Shylock out of his own long pocket," and put nothing into his plays but his own experience. True, Stephen ends this speech by saying, ". . . let some meinherr from Almany grope his life long for deephid meanings in the depth of the buckbasket."

But in spite of this warning we must go further with Joyce's work than the search for the biographical details on which it is usually founded. For when he began to turn the piece of experience which had aroused his imagination into a piece of writing, he frequently searched for some other writer's work to use as a sort of literary scaffolding for his own structure. It is with *Finnegans Wake* that this is most noticeable, and Joyce once wrote to Miss Weaver, ". . . such an amount of reading seems to be necessary before my old flying machine grumbles into the air."[36] But the use of the rhythm from Bret Harte's *Gabriel Conroy,* which has already been pointed out, is just one kind of borrowing for a structural purpose. Stanislaus Joyce has told us that the story "Grace" is based on the pattern "Inferno, Purgatorio, Paradiso" from Dante. The Homeric parallel underlying *Ulysses* is the unescapable example of such a basis, and it has been suggested by Richard Levin and Charles Shattuck that *Dubliners* itself has a similar Homeric basis. This may well be so, but the value of this basis, if it exists—which has been frequently disputed—would be in the satisfaction it gave to Joyce by providing an orderly framework on which to arrange what might seem to him otherwise incoherent material. The actual connections are so tenuous that a reader gains nothing in his appreciation of the stories by considering them. But having obtained, in some way that suited his own purpose, a structural basis, Joyce then provided a superimposed network of significant details which could be elevated into symbols, and which produce an effect of unity and order that repays study by enhancing the reader's appreciation of the work as a whole. Perhaps the chief group of symbols is that concerned with illusion and reality, which recurs constantly throughout the stories. Their intention is furthered by a series of statements about outward appearances which are deceptive. In the first paragraph of "The Sisters": "I had thought his words idle. Now I knew they were true." At the beginning of "An Encounter": "The peaceful odour of Mrs. Dillon was prevalent in the hall of the house. But he played too fiercely for us . . . ." And: "Everyone was incredulous when . . . . Nevertheless it was true." The houses in the first paragraph of "Araby" were "conscious of decent lives within them as they gazed at one another with brown imperturbable faces," but inside "Air, musty from having been long enclosed, hung in all the rooms, and the waste room behind the kitchen was littered with old useless papers." Similar examples could be collected from all the other stories; I have used only the first three.

Almost invariably Joyce succeeds in using as a symbol an actual object which he is also using as a literally meaningful detail in a naturalistic description. Only occasionally do we have such a passage as that in which the little boy who is the hero of "Araby" carries the image of his friend's sister through the Dublin crowds and tells us, "I imagined that I bore my chalice safely through a throng of foes." This, however, is the usual "Symbolist" practice. Joyce's effectiveness as a writer comes partly from his fusion of the naturalistic and symbolist techniques.

More important as a factor in producing that effect of weight and force which all Joyce's stories possess was his conviction that they represented situations which were truly representative. He wrote about the city he knew and the people he knew, but he believed that this city and people were like all other cities and people, and that the more precisely he depicted their idiosyncracies the more universal their application became. He was, as he makes Stephen say in *Stephen Hero,* releasing "from the vestment of its appearance" the essence of the human situation. "The poet . . . alone is capable of absorbing in himself the life that surrounds him and of flinging it abroad again amid planetary music." This statement, which Joyce makes in both his essay on Mangan and in *Stephen Hero,* was used by Kristian Smidt to support his thesis that Joyce elevated his own writing into the status of a religion.[37] In *Finnegans Wake* Shem, who is basically Joyce as a writer, "the penman," speaks of "reflecting from his own individual person life unlivable, transaccidentated through the slow fires of consciousness into a dividual chaos, perilous, potent, common to allflesh, human only, mortal."[38] Shem then goes on to talk about the individual stories of *Dubliners*. It is this belief in his own daemon, his own determination, which makes his work so effective that, as he wrote of Mangan, "one cannot but discern some fierce energy beneath the banter."[39]

Fortified by his conviction of the importance of his own genius, Joyce, as he wrote *Dubliners*, was establishing for himself a persona, discovering and developing a technique—or, rather, a whole armory of techniques—and deciding upon his attitude to Dublin and to life. He was to deal with all of life. Ellmann remarks that Joyce's original plan for the book shows him "seeing the city of Dublin itself as a person, with four stages of life to be represented, the first by its children, the last by its settled figures." To support this he quotes a letter by Joyce: "The order of the stories is as follows. *The Sisters, An Encounter* and another story *Araby* which are stories of my childhood: *The Boarding House, After the Race* and *Eveline*, which are stories of adolescence: *The Clay, Counterparts* and *A Painful Case* which are stories of mature life; *Ivy Day in the Committee Room, A Mother* and the last story in the book, *Grace*, which are stories of public life in Dublin." If Ellmann's suggestion is correct, and it seems to be, then there is a remarkable similarity in intention between *Dubliners* and *Finnegans Wake*, particularly when we remember that Joyce added a last story, "The Dead," which ends with an evocation of the union of "all the living and the dead."

Joyce's interpreters have frequently, and sometimes justly, been attacked for finding too many subtleties of implication in his works, but if we consider a remark made by a critic about another equally dedicated writer, then Joyce's critics seem justified. *"When a reader finds that his poet considers himself responsible for every syllable not simply in this or that poem but in every poem of his entire works, then his alertness is intensified, his curiosity aroused, his trust increased."* This comment by Geoffrey Tillotson, in *On the Poetry of Pope*,[40] applies with equal force to the work of Joyce which was pondered over and revised with a scrupulosity quite equal to that of Pope. As a parallel to Tillotson's remarks, it is relevant to consider one of the first critical comments ever made on the short story: Poe's statement, in his review of Hawthorne's *Twice-Told Tales,* that the short story should "contain no word of which the tendency direct or indirect, is not to the pre-established design." With these two points in mind—that every word has been pondered over, and that the form is one in which every word must perform a function—the danger becomes apparent of dismissing as inapplicable any explanation of Joyce's work purely on the grounds that it is oversubtle or farfetched.

Marvin Magalaner points out that "Throughout the story, 'Grace,' Joyce seems to be drawing a parallel between the Dublin police force and the Dublin priesthood. . . . The clergy, Joyce seems to feel, are no more delicate and sensitive in the administering of their trust than the constabulary of theirs. The crowded pub is paralleled by the crowded church," and so on, the "immense constable" being paralleled by the "massive" Father Purdon, as is stressed by both kneeling, and one drawing off a glove and the other drawing back his sleeves. Magalaner ends by saying: "If these supposed similarities are coincidental and not the result of a deliberately drawn comparison and contrast, then it is difficult to explain much of the rambling conversation about policemen and priests."[41] A careful reading of the story leaves one in no doubt about the accuracy of Magalaner's remarks. But in another story, "Clay," it seems to me that Magalaner has found more significance than Joyce intended. He sees the central figure, Maria, both as a witch—because it is Halloween when witches have their outing, and because when she laughed "the tip of her nose nearly met the tip of her chin"—and also, for various reasons, as the Virgin Mary. In a broadcast on the B.B.C., afterwards printed in *The Listener,* March 25, 1954, Stanislaus Joyce attacked Magalaner, although without actually naming him, for this suggestion. Magalaner reprinted Stanislaus Joyce's remarks in *James Joyce, the Man, the Work, the Reputation,* and defended his opinion adding only, "Perhaps he [James Joyce] has not sufficiently reinforced the relationship between the witch and the Virgin."[42] It seems more likely that Joyce never thought of Maria as a type of the Virgin Mary.

The real danger of this sort of analogy-tracing is not, however, the invention of nonexistent analogies but the withdrawal of attention from the real merit of Joyce's stories. They have—in spite of the vaunted "odour of corruption"—a liveliness and air of reality. The characters are convincing; their conversations sound real. Most fictional characters taken from real life are wooden and unconvincing, with an unpredictability of action that betrays their origin. Joyce's are surprisingly life-like. Perhaps he was saved here by his frequent custom of basing his characters on more than one real person—usually *himself* and one other. Mr. Duffy, of "A Painful Case"—for example—is Stanislaus Joyce and James himself; Gabriel Conroy in "The Dead" wrote for the same paper as James Joyce but makes after-dinner speeches like his father. He thus put himself into the characters he described in two ways, by including traits of his own and by transforming them "through the slow fires of consciousness," to quote his phrase from *Finnegans Wake* again. What he is doing is what Coleridge once advised himself to do: "Mix up truth and imagination"; Coleridge hoped that in this way reality might "spread its sense of substance and distinctness to imagination."[43] Joyce's aim seems to have been to enlarge the individual example he is describing into a universal type, all the more convincing because of its basis in individuality.

The point of view is manipulated with unobstrusive deftness. In "Counterparts" for example, we look at events as Farrington sees them, and then find ourselves observing disapprovingly his "dirty eyes." Little Chandler, in "A Little Cloud," is clearly portrayed, from outside, as an immature, ineffectual figure, but the story begins with four pages in which we are aroused to sympathy with him by seeing through his eyes and sharing his thoughts. In "The Boarding House" the prose suddenly drops into vulgarity to tell us that we are seeing things in the mercenary way in which Mrs. Mooney, "the Madam," sees them: "She knew he had a good screw for one thing, and she suspected he had a bit of stuff put by." For the first three stories we remain carefully focused, observing from the narrator's viewpoint with a child's eyes. Not until the last paragraph of the fourth story, "Eveline," does the viewpoint change; there, after the events have been narrated we reach, as usual at the end of a work by Joyce, a moment of stasis; and we see Eveline from outside, dispassionately: "She set her white face to him, passive, like a helpless animal. Her eyes gave him no sign of love or farewell or recognition."

Joyce's ability to write lifelike dialogue is a feature of all his books. In the density of *Finnegans Wake* characters appear and vanish, to reappear again and be immediately recognizable by their way of talking; *Ulysses* is full of lively talkers, each with his own voice. The dialogue in *Dubliners* is not as good as that in the later books, but already it is admirable. Here again, Joyce's method of turning his experience into fiction is noticeable. Mr. Henchy, of "Ivy Day in the Committee Room," speaks with the unmistakable accents of John Joyce, or Simon Dedalus: "there's a certain little nobleman with a cock-eye—you know the patriot I'm alluding to?" Lenehan of "Two Gallants" recurs in his own name in the Aeolus chapter of *Ulysses* where he is used to add many of the rhetorical figures which symbolize its "art," but his manner of speech in *Dubliners* is less developed. We recognize him by one remark: "Of all the good ones ever I heard, he said, that emphatically takes the biscuit." It is "the solitary, the recherché biscuit" in *Ulysses*. Eliza's last speech in "The Sisters" shows Joyce's ability to establish an individual and convincing sentence structure and rhythm as a means of character portrayal. The repetitions and simple sentences and childlike connectives serve not only to complete the picture of the somewhat dull Eliza but also to provide the required atmosphere for the denouement of the story: "So one night he was wanted for to go on a call and they couldn't find him anywhere. They looked high up and low down; and still they couldn't see a sight of him anywhere. So then the clerk suggested to try the chapel. So then they got the keys . . ." and so on until the end of the story: "So then, of course, when they saw that, that made them think that there was something wrong with him." Perhaps "the clerk suggested" strikes a false note—"the clerk said" might fit better—but the rest of the speech is perfectly adjusted to its purposes.

Before leaving Joyce's dialogue in *Dubliners,* I would like to draw special attention to one minor feature. Alone of Joyce's published works it has the dialogue in quotation marks. This was not Joyce's intention. It is the result of the printer's interference with the first edition, and of slavish imitation in subsequent printings. Joyce wrote to Grant Richards: "As for the appearance of the book I am content to leave it to your judgment . . . . On one point I would wish you to be careful. I would like your printer to follow the manuscript accurately in punctuation and arrangement. Inverted commas, for instance, to enclose dialogue always seemed to me a great eyesore."[44] Not until Joyce became an accepted writer was he able to impose this condition successfully. I think the time has now arrived for some publisher to produce *Dubliners* as Joyce wished it to appear.

Little has been said of the formal structure of Joyce's stories.

The Joyce of *Dubliners*

A short story must have a beginning in which the characters and, usually, their background are presented; a development—more or less involved—in which the characters do something or something happens to them; and an end resolving in some way the problems raised by the first two parts. The specific quality, the subtle force, which characterizes Joyce as a writer is most evident in the conclusions of his works. The "yes" of *Ulysses* is famous; *Finnegans Wake* ends with "the"—a word which Joyce said was a mere escaping of breath, but which conceals the title of the goddess: *Thea*. The *Dubliners* stories all end at a moment of stasis, often with an ironic tinge. "I will set right my accounts", at the end of "Grace," leaves the reader certain that the accounts will not be set right and that the materialism which is masquerading as religion presents no final answer. The final irony can point in many directions. The end of "Ivy Day in the Committee Room" is "Mr Crofton said it was a very fine piece of writing." The emotion which had been expressed by the writing was genuine; the events which had aroused that emotion were of historic importance; only the expression of the emotion was inadequate, but it is this which is singled out for praise. The final sentence of "The Boarding House" is "Then she remembered what she had been waiting for." This, as Hugh Kenner has pointed out,[45] leaves the story at its exact point of balance. It is a flat, undistinguished prose sentence, completely without emotion, without rhythm. Its colorlessness provokes the reader to stand back and consider dispassionately the circumstances detailed in the story. At the opposite pole is the famous closing paragraph of "The Dead" with its elegiac rhythm demanding that the reader shall share the writer's emotional involvement. Equally effective on a smaller scale is the closing sentence of "Araby" with its alliterative emphasis of the rhythm: "driven and derided . . . anguish and anger." Each of the endings brings out the full flavour of the story it concludes.

The openings of the stories vary considerably. "The Sisters" untypically begins at the end with the death of the priest and then works back to establish the events. Several stories begin in the manner of a formal dramatic comedy with minor characters who set the scene. "Ivy Day in the Committee Room," "The Dead" and "A Mother" are of this type. Set descriptions of the scene begin "Two Gallants" and "Araby," but in both stories the function of the settings is ironic. A few paragraphs introducing the chief character against his normal background may be considered the standard form for a short story's opening. This method is used for "A Painful Case," "Eveline" and "Counterparts," but in each case Joyce is also setting the tone and the atmosphere. This can, of course, be done without introducing main characters—*Hamlet* is the conspicuous example of this method—but the short story rarely has room for the method. Joyce tries it once, in "An Encounter," where Joe Dillon has no real connection with the plot but dominates the opening paragraphs.

Each story has its own distinctive formal structure. Perhaps "Counterparts" comes closest to the typical short story with its introduction of the chief character at the opening, and a parallel in that character's son at the end. The force of Joyce's indignation, felt much more here than elsewhere, gives the story its strength. Perhaps the most unusual story, as to the structural technique employed, is "A Little Cloud." The story is about Little Chandler's failure to live; Joyce begins with the emphasis on Gallaher (the successful journalist whom we meet later in *Ulysses*), but he weaves his two parts together so skillfully that the story remains a unity.

It would be interesting to examine the development of all the stories but this would take a book at least as long as the stories themselves. One story will have to serve as an example for all, even though it must be stressed that Joyce used a different method of development for each story. Sometimes, as with "Grace," the basic pattern of the story is taken from a literary source; the three parts of "Grace" are based on the Hell, Purgatory and Inferno of Dante's *Divine Comedy*. This basis, which probably helped Joyce when writing his story, adds nothing to its literary value or the reader's enjoyment. But Joyce's assumption at least, should never be forgotten. For example, many critics have discussed the relevance of the verses Little Chandler reads from Byron, but none of them has pointed out that Chandler reads the first verses on the first page of Byron's collected poems, verses which Byron himself apologized for including in his juvenilia. This gives a stress which could hardly be strengthened to the portrayal of Chandler as immature; but no one seems to have noticed.

The story I have chosen to examine as a whole is "The Boarding House," mainly because this is an average sort of story which nobody has ever said was better or worse than the rest of *Dubliners*. As a first glance the plot is simple enough. It is when one tries to summarize it that the wealth of detail becomes evident: Mr. Doran, a respectable, bespectacled clerk in a prominent Catholic wine store, has seduced his landlady's daughter, Polly Mooney. Mrs. Mooney, a butcher's daughter, had married her father's foreman, and they opened their own shop; but her father died and her husband took to drink and "went for his wife with the cleaver," so Mrs. Mooney had set up on her own in a boarding house while her husband became "a shabby stooped little drunkard" with the most despised of all occupations in the Dublin of those days—that of sheriff's man, whose duty was to deliver summonses and collect debts. But Mrs. Mooney, "a big imposing woman," managed her house "cunningly and firmly." Besides Polly she has a son, Jack, who now works in a bookie's office. Like his mother he is powerfully built; he looks dangerous and is handy with his fists. Mrs. Mooney, who has quietly watched the events between Polly and

Mr. Doran, chooses a moment when Jack is around to speak to Mr. Doran about it. He promises to marry Polly.

The details are all made significant and used to build up a complete and integrated situation; as L.A.G. Strong once said, "A *tour de force* of technique, this story shifts the interest from mother to young man, and finally to daughter, without breaking its unity."[46] It is, indeed, the order of presentation which is surprising. The first paragraph contains enough information about Mrs. Mooney and her husband to provide the ground plan for a novel, and—unlike the bald account I have just given—it is very readable, fulfilling efficiently one purpose of an opening paragraph by catching the reader's interest. The undesirable husband at loose in Dublin provides a reason for keeping Polly at home,—with, of course, the aim of marriage to a boarder. The brother is available to suggest the threat of physical force at a suitable moment. Only when the situation has been established are we shown Mr. Doran. He is "very anxious indeed this Sunday morning." He has been to confession the night before and is thinking about it. So Joyce, with the neatest possible arrangement of retrospective narration, tells us how the seduction happened and leaves us in doubt whether Polly or Mr. Doran did the seducing. The artistry of the end has already been discussed. We are spared Mrs. Mooney's recriminations and remain pleasantly occupied upstairs in the bedroom with Polly who is letting her memories give place "to hopes and visions."

Of the characters, only Mrs. Mooney can be said to have any real personality; the others remain flat, and yet are adequate within the bounds of the story. The background is so vivid, the focus of presentation is so deep, that the little story has the air of reality. Behind the story, giving it its energy, is Joyce's urge to portray precisely the city he knew, in all its meanness. And for him the situation was a typical one. Mrs. Mooney, helped by her name, reappears in *Finnegans Wake* as the moon whose nymphs were created to entrap the sons of men. "There where the missers moony,"[47] shows us Joyce still remembering her. He was still sure, as he always had been, that the situations he wrote about were important, and that his writing was important. With these convictions all that one needs to become a great writer is genius and the capacity for taking pains—and these too he had.

4

A PORTRAIT OF THE ARTIST AS A YOUNG MAN: AFTER FIFTY YEARS

William T. Noon, S.J.

I

A Portrait of the Artist as a Young Man was first published from London in the *Egoist* magazine. Ezra Pound sponsored its publication and transmitted installments of about fifteen pages each to the editor. It ran serially, with a few breaks, from February 2, 1914, James Joyce's thirty-second birthday, until September 1, 1915. Substantially the same text was used when it was first published in book form December 29, 1916, by B. W. Huebsch, New York, as is pointed out by John Slocum and Herbert Cahoon in their *Bibliography*.[1] Peter Spielberg more recently has shown that most of the errors that had crept into the first editions of 1914-1915 and 1916 persisted for nearly half a century. They have re-occurred until lately in all subsequent American printings (Modern Library, Compass Books, Viking Portable, and so on), and also in almost all conveniently available editions and translations abroad.[2] Since some of the errors are significant, and since Joyce himself "carefully prepared a list of errata in April, 1917,"[3] it is regrettable that the many readers of *A Portrait* and the many commentators on it were obliged for so long to make do with a faulty text.

It is now fortunate in this half-centenary year of *A Portrait's* first publication as a book that we have at last not just one but two carefully corrected and emended texts, each modestly priced and each readily available. Chester G. Anderson and Richard Ellmann in 1964 provided a definitive text corrected from the Dublin Holograph of *A Portrait,* a Compass Book of the Viking Press, New York; and James S. Atherton later in the same year furnished a carefully researched and revised text (based also in part on the Dublin Holograph) brought out in the Modern Novel Series by Heinemann Educational Books, London. Here, in a sense, is an embarrassment of riches!

Atherton's presentation of *A Portrait* is in some ways the more helpful of these two recent editions because he gives us not only a clear text of the novel but also an economical and readable Biographical Note on the author, a literate Introduction to the novel for students or returning readers; and some twenty well-arranged pages, at the end, of valuable, refreshing and seldom-enough-adverted-to but necessary Notes. Since most readers of Joyce meet him for the first time in literature courses that include *A Portrait,* the usefulness of the Atherton-Heinemann text is of considerable consequence. American commentators on *A Portrait,* however, will probably still be obliged to quote and note from the Compass Book edition since the Viking Press more than ten years ago in this country took back its copyright rights, and now exercises them for *A Portrait,* both in the Compass Book and Viking Portable editions.

As Spielberg shows in his article on Errata, *A Portrait* is today a literary classic, widely read, much commented on, often reprinted. I do not know the statistics of publication for all of Joyce's works, but I expect that *A Portrait* is the one most widely read. All bibliographies of scholarly studies in literature include items about this book in ever-accelerating frequency: *PMLA, Review of English Studies, Modern Fiction Studies, Abstracts of English Studies, Cambridge Bibliography of English*

Literature, Modern Language Review, International Index, and so forth. The *James Joyce Quarterly* (which began publication in 1963) now often carries an extended "Supplemental JJ Checklist" by Alan M. Cohn, sometimes with Richard M. Kain. *The James Joyce Review* (discontinued in 1959) used formerly to carry with some regularity entries in "James Joyce Studies" by William White. All these lists include innumerable items about *A Portrait*. So does Robert H. Deming's *A Bibliography of James Joyce Studies,* No. 18 in the Library Series of the University of Kansas Publications, 1964. The Special Number "James Joyce" of *Modern Fiction Studies,* way back (so it now seems) in 1958, carried a long selected checklist by Maurice Beebe and Walton Litz of special studies of Joyce's separate works. This highly selective, partial list includes nearly two finely printed pages of recommended titles on *A Portrait*. There has been no dearth in the making of books and articles about *A Portrait,* and there is no end in view. Here now comes another!

Some of these articles and books are stimulated artificially, to be sure, as it were from on high, by Joyce's present-day towering position in the Academy, or "Establishment" (as that Academy is often referred to and refers to itself). How Joyce might have smiled! Some of this artificial stimulation is forced or fostered by the hothouse environment of certain schools, colleges, graduate department, where Joyce's works are highly privileged touchstones of a literary student's or a professor's competence. Joycean expertise is a well-known trademark of scholarly industry. It tends to become an industry all by itself, establishing its own monopoly of experts. It looks at times as though it might become a swindle.

In Mary McCarthy's *The Groves of Academe* (1952), it is said of Henry Mulcahy, a Joycean expert and the central character in this much-troubled, witty story: "He believes that he's been subject to persecution for propagating the Word. This, he insists, is at the bottom of his troubles . . . . He is hated, he says, by Joyce's enemies, who comprise the whole academic world, with the exception of rival Joyce experts who hate him also, since they are really Joyce's enemies in disguise."[4] There is an explosive danger for the life and limbs of literature when men or women with such obsessions take over the rule of any grove in the world academic. It is now 1966, and the Henry Mulcahys now call the tunes of this grove even more often than they did in 1952.

In the long run, however, propaganda of any sort tends to ricochet on its perpetrators. A kind of defensive solemnity, a being too much on guard, manifests itself in some current Joycean criticism. Nor is the literacy of all of it of a high order. In fairness one needs to add that a generous proportion of it *is* well-written, though quantity outruns quality in some of it: a kind of cosmic free-wheeling in space. Joyce himself was a creative literary artist, not a professional scholar. He brooded much, however, over his ideas: how as an artist he might make them his own, how he might then express them imaginatively so as to make them sound original and personal. So, after his brooding and blending, they most often did. He revised and much re-revised all that he wrote.

Scholarly criticism too has its creative side. It is unrealistic to maintain that critics are all frustrated artists. But even writing creative scholarly criticism is not the same as writing fiction, nor as rewriting someone else's book. Interpretative analysis here is helpful when it enables a reader to note Joyce's fresh manner of speaking, or to understand more clearly and sympathetically some important idea, image, or analogue that is hinted at but not spelled out in Joyce's admittedly allusive text. But professors of literature run a double risk of talking a good book like *A Portrait* to death. Being bookish persons, they may sometimes show themselves to be, as it were, over-perceptive. Some published comment on this book of Joyce's might also to its advantage take a more relaxed tone. Joyceans by and large are good-natured, intelligent scholars, helpful to one another and to those for whom they speak or write. Even they grow tired of being talked at by some of their humanist colleagues who speak with an edge in their voice. Our twentieth century at all levels, humanist and religious included, is already cluttered with impersonal apostles of personalism.

But the prestige-symbol value of *A Portrait* does not explain its whole story. This book must have something vital still to say to modern minds and imaginations, and Joyce must here still say it in an arresting way, if one is to account for this book of his being so much written about, possibly over-written about today. Why is Joyce "in" when so many of his peers are now "out"? Literary fads come and go. But Joyce goes on. . . . In spite of Establishments and Academies, a book or author cannot for over fifty years hold literary stature as a classic against the will of the people who read. Young people, in particular—all, at their best, experimentalists—know what they like and value, and they are not inarticulate in letting their seniors know what values and likes they intend to make prevail. They are coming up all the time into the "Establishments." And at this most outspoken moment, 1966, and after fifty years, Joyce's *A Portrait* is still a widely prevailing book.

Two recent paperbacks that are making their way without difficulty suggest that many young men and women read with some eagerness, or at least readiness, not only *A Portrait* but also books about it. For example, William E. Morris' and Clifford A. Nault's Odyssey Press Casebook, *Portraits of an Artist* (1962), and Thomas E. Connolly's Goldentree Book, *Joyce's "Portrait": Criticisms and Critiques* (also, 1962). Both of these are textbooks, selections of critical essays. Both are helpful threads through the labyrinth of Joyce's mind as far as 1916. They indicate, for instance, Stephen Dedalus, in *A Portrait,* as a kind of alter ego of Joyce. His mind reflects Joyce's and

Ireland's at the turn of the century,—that is, "as we were." But Stephen is also a fictional character, created by Joyce, and Stephen's mind has its own special twists and turnings. Any guidebook or map that is completely drawn can help the uninitiated adventurer to make his way through Joyce's "forest of symbols" and across Stephen Dedalus's stream-of-consciousness. Still, each adventurer needs to take his own journey, make his own report. A traveller does not just look at maps.

The essays, maps or diagrams, selected by Morris and Nault are more numerous, more extensively trimmed and edited, have more insets than those by Connolly, and they are more explicitly arranged, drawn or designed, for classroom use. They present views more varied, sometimes contradictory views. In these two collections there are, of course, some overlappings, duplications and repetitions. Comments on the aesthetic theories of *A Portrait* take up one hundred and twenty pages in the Connolly collection, whereas the Morris-Nault collection devotes about seventy pages to them. Both texts provide selective bibliographies, and both pose questions for further reflection and discussion so as to help readers make up their own minds. Robert S. Ryf has given his book *A New Approach to Joyce* (1962) the subtitle "The Portrait of the Artist as a Guidebook," that is, an aid for travellers through the complete Joycean (or Dedalan) maze.

Ideally, every true Joycean supposes, a reader of *A Portrait* should also have already read or be in the act of reading straight through all of Joyce's works, the published ones certainly, the unpublished as far as access may be secured to them. Each successive work of Joyce presupposes familiarity with all that have gone before. The early Stephen Dedalus sections of *Ulysses,* the first three episodes that are called *Telemachia,* are almost unintelligible for a reader who lacks familiarity with the introspective workings of Stephen Dedalus's mind in *A Portrait.* Finally *Finnegans Wake* assumes a knowledge of *Ulysses, A*

Portrait, Dubliners, and so forth. For example, in the *Wake* both the "Mime of Mick Nick and the Maggies" (Bk. II, ch. 1) and "The Fable of the Ondt and the Gracehoper" (Bk. III, ch. 1) would lose much of their fun for the *Wake*-reader who failed to recognize that these two parables are burlesque variations on Joyce's own quasi-autobiographical story of *A Portrait.*

But seldom are the Joycean's ideals, or anybody else's, altogether practicable. Most readers of *A Portrait* are not Joycean experts. Few, in fact, are specialists in any author. Nevertheless, the continuing independent interest in this relatively simple story suggests that it can be read not just for its story but also for its own built-in interpretation of that story, without further need of glosses from other works of fiction or from overmuch commentary by experts. The experts have variously described this story as a *Kunstlerroman* (that is, the story of the growth or development of an artist's, a poet's mind), a *Bildungsroman* (the story, or shape, of any young person's development), and a *Geistesroman* (the story of a life of the mind).

So far as these German labels are accurate (they appear to be), any reader's understanding and evaluation of *A Portrait* should be helped, not hindered, by knowing that this quasi-autobiographical fiction is the third version, at least, that Joyce wrote of it. The earliest known draft, or copy, of *A Portrait of the Artist* (simply so entitled) is a short essay, closely written on ruled paper, that in its later, typed, form is among the documents acquired in 1957 by the Cornell University Library from the estate of Stanislaus Joyce, James Joyce's brother. Richard M. Kain and Robert E. Scholes have edited this original draft of Joyce's "Portrait," and their edition of it was first published in *The Yale Review* in 1960.[5] "A portrait is not an identificative paper but the curve of an emotion": so in part reads this copybook essay. Kain and Scholes (presumably on the basis of the holograph) date it January 7, 1904. It runs to about two and a half sheets in Stanislaus's typescript copy, six and a half pages in *The Yale Review* published text. Kain and Scholes begin their Introduction to this text with the information that the original copy was written at the close of Joyce's twenty-first year—that would be, then, late 1902 or early 1903—and they describe this prose work of some two thousand words as "part manifesto, part narrative." So it is, although the large manifesto tells one more than does the slight narrative about Joyce's idea of a portrait as "an individuating rhythm," a "diagnosis," "a fluid succession of presents."

Joyce's second known version of *A Portrait* is the by now well-known *Stephen Hero*. This second version, however, was scarcely known to exist at all until Theodore Spencer came across a handwritten copy of about a quarter of the manuscript among the Sylvia Beach papers acquired by the Harvard College Library in 1938. Spencer meticulously edited this partial version of what Joyce had provisionally entitled *Stephen Hero,* and New Directions published his edition in 1944 as "A Part of the First Draft of *A Portrait of the Artist as a Young Man.*"[6] Since this preserved part of Joyce's early draft runs to 383 manuscript pages and yet covers only a part of the concluding period of life covered in *A Portrait* (in some ninety printed pages), it is evident that Joyce here drastically reduced the length of his story in the re-telling of it. Nor, evidently, were all his changes just for the sake of compression. Between this early, projected story, *Stephen Hero,* and Joyce's final, finished story, *A Portrait,* there have been a considerable number of rethinkings and reworkings of his materials as to episodes, phrasings, and tones. Some thirty or so additional manuscript pages for *Stephen Hero* (most, not all of them, a continuation of Spencer's first "find") have turned up since Spencer edited his first text in 1944. These are all now incorporated into the 1963 version with five additional pages of the *Stephen Hero* that is available in a New Directions paperback text. Understandably, any editor needs to adopt some conjectures of his own as to just what the youthful Joyce might have wished left in or taken out of his much-slashed, much marked-up (and until 1944) unpublished text.

There is some uncertainty as to just when Joyce first began to tell his *Stephen Hero* story: was it back in Dublin in 1901-1902 (as I think likely from reference to it in still unpublished family letters), or after he left Dublin in 1904? There are greater uncertainties, many apocryphal stories by no means agreeing among themselves, as to just what might have happened to the many still missing pages of this *Stephen Hero* manuscript. No one really knows for sure. If one takes Joyce's own word, he himself later on did not think highly of this early draft of *A Portrait*. It is diffuse; Stephen takes himself too seriously, his biases at times are starchy, at times dour; his heroic-mindedness and artistic inclinations are a bit too much on the adolescent side. Stephen Daedalus (as Stephen's last name is spelled in *Stephen Hero*) later on appeared to Joyce as a young man too much lost in his own labyrinth ("You is feeling like you was lost in the bush, boy?" *FW*, 112).[7] "And what rubbish it is," so Joyce in 1934 wrote to Harriet Shaw Weaver, whom he much respected and to whom he usually said what he meant.[8]

If "rubbish it is," it is a piece highly prized, that scholars have gone to great pains in the past twenty years to polish and burnish so that it might shine. Spencer was the first to note that this "schoolboy's production" (Joyce's phrase for it) has value both extrinsic and intrinsic, that is, both as a preliminary draft of *A Portrait* and as an excellent literary sketch in its own right. Actually it is not easy to consider these two values separately. The commentator who has read both *Stephen Hero* and *A Portrait* tends forever afterwards to merge these two stories, to recall the one in the shadow of the other. In the finished work, *A Portrait*, the virtues of intensity, focus, and design are certainly clearer. But, as Spencer notes in his Preface, *Stephen Hero* shows qualities of excellence that to the same degree are missing from the finished work: freshness or starkness of detail, candor and vividness of personal observation, narrative simplicity and directness in showing more sharply what concerns most mattered in Stephen's life of the mind. Stephen's biases are clearer in the *Stephen Hero* draft. So too are the conflicts that engage his soul and body from within and from without.

Not a few of the narrative episodes that are obscure in *A Portrait* take on a clear enough sense of form and direction when one reads them in *Stephen Hero's* light: for example, the identity of E. C., Emma Clery, the rather plain girl with forced manners, whose image Stephen in *A Portrait* radiantly transsubstantiates (so he says) into an artistic Eucharist, "the temptress of his villanelle" (220-224, Compass Edition); the reason for Stephen's special dislike of Father Moran, "suave priest," who, he suspects, has been flirting with Emma; the troubled sense of dependence that Stephen as a young man feels on his pious Irish mother's high regard, even when in *Stephen Hero* he more than once pitilessly unnerves her and bluntly blames her for infecting him with the contagion that has paralyzed, so he says, all of Dublin's motor centers of the brain. In *A Portrait,* Stephen's narrative indictment of Dublin is just as thoroughgoing and defiant, but he shows less hysteria, especially less at the end as he goes away. The banners of rebellion are at the end still flying in *A Portrait,* but the later young man senses the cost, confesses his lack of heart, questions the self, and calculates the risks (252-253, 247, 240-241) more humanly than the earlier Stephen is ever disposed to do. Still it is in *Stephen Hero,* not in *A Portrait,* that Stephen answers Cranly's question as to why he left the Church, by saying, "I could not observe the precepts" (140). In both versions, Cranly is a close confidant of Stephen's, but in the *Stephen Hero* version his role is larger and more sharply defined, as a kind of Father Confessor for Stephen. In an early clothbound notebook of Joyce's now at the Cornell University Library, Joyce identifies

Cranly as John Francis Byrne (the author of *The Silent Years,* 1953) and says of him, "He hears confessions without giving absolution: a guilty priest" (see also, *A Portrait,* 178).

As critiques of *A Portrait* almost endlessly demonstrate, its aesthetic theories cannot now be fully paraphrased or interpreted without many references back to *Stephen Hero*. Everyone now tries in the light of such references to define just what Stephen in *A Portrait* appears to mean. There is, of course, some sleight-of-hand usually hidden in such a critical enterprise, since Joyce between 1902 (or 1904) and 1915-1916, "away from home," presumably may on some points have enlarged or changed his own—even Stephen's—mind. These theories of art are expressed at greater length in *Stephen Hero* than in *A Portrait*. There is less drama in their earlier presentation, and they are not mixed with a built-in qualification by way of wry irony or humor (Lynch's coarse interruptions in *A Portrait*).

One by now quasi-rubrical imperative of Joycean aesthetics, the "Epiphany," is altogether suppressed in *A Portrait*. For *Stephen Hero* this rubric has come to be attended to in a highly privileged way. One recent commentator, however, has said of this so-called Joycean concept of "Epiphany," as endlessly formulated and re-formulated by critics, that it is without meaning for Joyce's adult work (including, presumably, *A Portrait*). This same commentator likens "Epiphany-hunting" to Scrabble and expresses his wish that such an overworked, irrelevant rubric might now at last be "abandoned entirely."[9]

Some Joyceans might feel inclined to answer, or Joyce himself might have answered (who, however, knows?) that you do not *hunt* for epiphanies: that is the point, they reveal themselves! The observer, here the reader, is at some point jolted to a pause, or stasis, and wonders at the *being* of some commonplace. He marvels at the secret of some familiar person or idea or object that he has long seen but never really noticed before. "Claritas is quidditas."[10] In *Stephen Hero,* Stephen describes this clarity as an exquisite adjustment in focus on the part of the observer; it is, he says, the third and final, glowing "stage" in the mind's apprehension of beauty. The first stage is recognition; the second, analysis-synthesis; this third, final stage is a fleeting clarity of tone. The "soul" of the object or person so apprehended is said to be itself so exquisitely structured as to leap out. Beyond words, as it were, some worded being gives its whole secret away. Although Stephen illustrates his aesthetic ideas by the use of examples that are visible to the eye—a clock or a basket,—Joyce's own writing, as Stephen talks, voices auditory awareness that these revelations of being in literature come to readers through the ear. One hears or, better, overhears, what is being said. Stephen Dedalus, in *A Portrait*, does not talk about epiphany, but he speaks of this same claritas; he calls it "the enchantment of the heart" (213). Whatever may be the word used by Joyce or his critics, this heart-head apprehension appears to be part of the mystery of art. The intelligent mind always gladly recognizes the precedence of the reasons of the heart. The intuited reality here talked about would appear to be an ever-sounded note of all good literature, all the more so of any that introspectively is being played by and for the ear.

The source itself for Joyce's literary term "epiphany" has been long sought and variously identified. The source closest to Joyce, of course, is the Catholic liturgy: the silent grace that empowered the Wise Men from the East to recognize God's hypostatic presence in the human Christ-child of Bethlehem. Joyce had abundant reason to know that this manifestation is recalled in Catholic liturgy with the major feast of January 6 each year. Other associations, Neoplatonic, mythical, theological, clustered in time around this Catholic image.[11] Stephen MacKenna, self-taught classicist, was working away in Dublin on his translations of *The Enneads* of Plotinus during the time that Joyce, not far away, was first drafting *Stephen Hero*. From his own attendance, Joyce knew about the conversational fireworks at MacKenna's memorable Saturday evenings at home.¹² Later, but before *A Portrait,* Joyce must have found out from his reading and from his Jewish friends in Trieste about the Jewish doctrine of the *Skeninah:* the glory of God, a majestic light and radiant manifestation that comes from some humble creature but points to the Almighty Creator Himself. These later variations on the Catholic liturgical core of meaning for "Epiphany" are mysterious in themselves, but not more so than is liturgy, and there is no reason to suppose that Joyce needed to learn about liturgy just from books. The poetic idea of Epiphany in *Stephen Hero* is an old and familiar one for literature, and in its own literary context it is rather clear and certainly striking. Whatever may have been Joyce's reasons in time for dropping the term or redirecting its sense, his later works illustrate often and poignantly the early core meaning that it once had in Stephen Dedalus' mind. It is a lyrical idea, to be sure, but then Joyce's later works are full of lyricism. They show better than might any discursive argument how careful the literary commentator needs to be in applying Stephen's "three forms progressing" (lyrical, epical, and dramatic, 213-214) to the story of Joyce's own development and progress. *Finnegans Wake* has often been described as a cerebral work; so, indeed, it is, but it is also on Stephen's own terms a more lyrical work than is *A Portrait.*

II

Now, as already suggested, in 1966 the big questions that one needs to ask about Joyce's *A Portrait of the Artist as a Young Man* are: Does this story still come through? Is it an important novel of spiritual growth? Of artistic and intellectual rebellion? Or is it a period piece? Has it been overread, overstudied? Is it outdated in its exotic concerns? Readers sometimes admire that which they do not like.

No one claims for *A Portrait* the same quality of classic,

enduring excellence that belongs unassailably to *Ulysses*. Nor might the usual reader who admires *A Portrait* and who has backed away from *Finnegans Wake* claim that Joyce's first novel has the even-now daring importance of his last major work. Is *A Portrait*, indeed, worth the close attention that most readers gladly give to Joyce's earlier *Dubliners* short stories?

I judge from my own experience with young readers, women and men, seminarians some, that for most *A Portrait* still speaks to them and is a story that most of them both admire and like. *A Portrait* shows movement, inside and outside the mind. It is not grounded as is the *Stephen Hero* fragment. Although Stephen in both versions follows a solitary path to his art, there is a note of artistic inevitability sounded in *A Portrait* that is not heard in the fragment. In both versions Stephen makes choices. But in the fragment one feels that although Stephen's life in Ireland was so lackluster he could have acted differently, whereas in *A Portrait* one feels that since his life in Ireland was this way Stephen had no other choice.

Most readers of *A Portrait* conclude that Stephen Dedalus is egocentric. At times he comes through as a kind of over-intellectualized pedant, as an esthete rather than as an artist. Or if an artist, at times he appears to be immature, a too easily wounded young man, like Richard Rowan in Joyce's play, *Exiles*. Richard, one feels, tries too hard to break all bonds, divine and human, including those of love. So one senses that his weary isolation at the end is owing to his own limitations. His "deep, deep wound of doubt" tires spectators just as much as it tires Richard.

Stephen Dedalus is also an intelligently sensitive young man. He is supremely dedicated to his art. Only at the end of the story does he feel obligated to withdraw from his society. He concludes at the start, however, that it is a too much settled, sick society. He concludes at the end that it can only paralyze all his artistic energies by those pressures that others have since come to call mass-cult and mass-mediocrity. His is a story of the loss of faith; it is also a story of the search for faith. And how might any story both of the loss of faith and the search for faith grow irrelevant in the twentieth century?

Stephen is searching for the good life: he wants to be whole. He hopes to be just. He is determined to be himself. *A Portrait* is certainly more than just a diatribe against turn-of-the-century Dublin society. As the title itself phrases it, this is the story of an *artist as a young man*. It is more than just a planned program of aesthetic rebellion and reform. Stephen is mixed-up, sometimes too readily injured or hurt. At the end, and in spite of his rhetoric, he realizes that he cannot replace God through the creative processes of literature, much as he might like to. Such, anyway, is Joyce's more mature point in this novel. At the end of *A Portrait,* Stephen pledges himself "to forge in the smithy of my soul the uncreated conscience of my race" (253). Even in this moment of withdrawal from Dublin, he is not forever renouncing all links. He has resolved to be more than just an Outsider, even as he goes away. He badly wants always to love the city that he is leaving behind. He remembers and recalls his mother's words to him as she packed his "new secondhand clothes" for his journey: "She prays now, she says, that I may learn in my own life and away from home and friends what the heart is and what it feels. Amen. So be it" (252).

The story of *A Portrait* unfolds symmetrically in five stages of Stephen Dedalus' spiritual development. The inner chapters, II, III, and IV, are mostly about his days in Belvedere College, a Jesuit high school for boys in the heart of Dublin. The first chapter is mostly about Stephen's experiences as a child, his first days in school at the then rather exclusive Jesuit boarding-school for boys, Clongowes Wood College, in County Kildare, not far from Dublin. The last chapter, V, the longest, is mostly about Stephen's college days at University College, also in Dublin, and at that time also conducted by the Jesuits. There are brief interludes elsewhere. In the first chapter there is one interlude that describes Stephen's troubled visit home to Dublin for Christmas; it presents the sad-glad Christmas dinner where sharp controversy about the fall of Charles Stewart Parnell bewilders young Stephen and extinguishes everyone's Christmas spirits. In the second chapter there are interludes that describe Stephen's holiday visits to Blackrock on the sea, and to Cork. These are both places where Joyce briefly lived with his family when he himself was a boy.

For each of these five chapters there is a more-or-less dominant image (or symbol), a rather pervasive emotion recollected, and at the end a rather marked pause, a stasis in the action of the story. As each chapter concludes, there is for Stephen a special, new kind of going away.

In Chapter I, the dominant image is Father Dolan's pandybat; the dominant emotion, a fear of grown-ups; and the pause of recollection, a sense of grateful relief at Father Arnall's taking his part. So it is as Stephen leaves childhood. In Chapter II, "a breakwater of order and elegance against the sordid tide of life without him" (98) variously serves as image; the guilt of the model schoolboy is the pervasive emotion (for already Stephen begins to doubt his religious faith); and "the swoon of sin" (101) in the brothel is the moment of stasis at the end. So he forsakes innocence and the life of sanctifying grace. In Chapter III, shortest of the chapters, Father Arnall's terrifying retreat-sermons on the punishment of the damned in hell—"fetid carcasses," "pain of intensity" (120, 130)—provide an image that is truly dominant; Stephen's emotion here is one of supernatural fright; the pause of recollection at the end describes Stephen's receiving the Holy Eucharist after he has made his retreat-confession. For the time being, at least, he goes away from a life of sin. In Chapter IV, there occurs what is probably the dominant image of the whole book, Stephen's vision (part sight, part imagination) of the young wading girl in the stream; the dominant emotion is that of profane joy for the "hawklike man" in his recognition of his true vocation, to be not a priest at the altar but a priest of the eternal imagination (169, 171-172); here the stasis at the end describes Stephen's walk in the moonlight beside the sea. He knows that he has said "no" to his priestly calling: "On and on and on and on!" (172). In the concluding Chapter V, the dominant image is that of swallows (wild geese) in flight; the pervasive emotion, loneliness; the final stasis is Stephen's silent moment of poise just before flight. As absolutely as he may, he is about to go away from home.

A *Portrait* has, of course, literary antecedents. There is much uncertainty here, because Joyce was too much his own man for a commentator to state categorically just what these archetypes of the author might have been. The novel of spiritual development and of adolescent revolt is one that goes back at least as far as Samuel Butler's *The Way of All Flesh* (not published until 1903) and the various confessions of George Moore. It has roots in the French symbolists, and also in John Addington Symonds' many French-oriented volumes on the artists of the Renaissance and of Romanticism. In Germany, it has even earlier forebears in Goethe's *Werther* (1774, 1787) and *Dichtung und Wahrheit* (1831). This tradition includes, of course, and for Joyce especially, Newman's *Apologia* (1864) and, to be sure, Saint Augustine's *Confessions* (c. 400). There is already evidence available that Joyce had read all these books, or at least looked into them. How well in scholarly detail he might have known them is arguable. He probably read them hurriedly, as most artists are wont to read others' books. But he knew what was in the air! He had his own story to tell, and he ended up telling it in his own way. He had sense enough (in his mind, maybe not in his heart) to know that no artist's new way of telling a story ever catches on with others at once. There is always a time-lag. Modern minds are not nearly so modern as non-artists often imagine. With *A Portrait,* Joyce took his own risks.

As one looks back now on this story, it appears to be as much an elegy for a lost cause as it does a manifesto for the cause that its young man, an artist, proclaimed he would bring into being. *Forge* as a writer might by fabricating or counterfeiting, no artist *creates* consciences, certainly not for his entire race. God alone creates *ex nihilo sui et subjecti.* Men at their best can only hope to transform or modify. No young man can create a brand new world to suit his own tastes and specifications. God himself respects other persons' individual freedom of choice. Ireland (or Dublin) is now much different from what it was fifty years ago. Now, for example, it is proud to boast of James Joyce as a Dubliner, but its conscience is far from being the one that Stephen Dedalus promised to forge. By the time, indeed, that Joyce drew his final *Portrait* of Stephen Dedalus, he himself abroad had come to accept the situation in Dublin and all the human beings caught up in it with a wryly amused compassion. After all, 1916 was the year of the Easter Uprising, a Dublin happening that "transformed utterly" the comedy of life for all Dubliners, not just for W. B. Yeats. Francis Sheehey-Skeffington, Joyce's old friend of the University College days, was shot on the second day of that insurrection. In this story, *A Portrait,* already written before the Rising, Stephen may no longer think of himself as hero, but he still likes to play the role of pure and passive martyr: Stephen martyr, *Bous Stephanoumenos, Bous Stephaneferos* (168). He likes to think of himself as the sacrificial ox, the scapegoat, who bears his people's guilt but who also bears the poet's crown. Simon Dedalus is not the only one who is weeping for Parnell, his "uncrowned king," when the famous Christmas dinner scene in the first chapter of this novel comes to a close. So is Stephen! So are most readers. So, one supposes, was Joyce when he composed the scene. One also supposes that he smiled. *Lacrimae rerum:* the tears of things, and their absurdity too.

Joyce did not need in 1916 to look back so far through the haze at Stephen as we need to. Stephen is not altogether admirable, nor are any of these other Dubliners. With infinite pains Joyce tells their story well. It is mostly a tale of adolescent disillusionment. It is about the artistic aspiration of a young man to be self-possessed, self-achieving, self-aware. Stephen would like to be accepted by the world to which he belongs. This is usual enough. It is the kind of story that will probably never go out of date.

In reading *A Portrait,* the question of point-of-view needs to be answered. Although this novel is nowhere nearly so highly stylized a stream-of-consciousness as is *Ulysses* (1922), everything that happens in it comes to us filtered through the sensibility of Stephen Dedalus himself. Already Stephen's voice here begins to fade into the interior, withdrawn, at times barely audible monologue of a deeply introspective young man. How clear and fair a "reflector," or "center of consciousness" (to borrow Jamesian terms), are Stephen's imagination and mind? H. G. Wells is quoted on the back cover of the old 1956 Compass Book edition of *A Portrait* as saying (much earlier, in 1917), "it is by far the most living and convincing picture that exists of an Irish Catholic upbringing." Thomas Merton, a Catholic priest and a Trappist monk, in his *Secular Journal* (1959), spoke differently, in an entry under the date of February 18, 1940, when he was a young man: "It is too bad that he [Joyce] made the same mistake that the people who hate him have always made: that of making no distinction whatever between the culture of the Irish middle-class and the sacramental life of the Church."[13] Father Merton, I take it, assumes that James Joyce's "mistake" here is the same as Stephen's.

Any commentator on Joyce needs, to be sure, to know Catholicism if he wants to find out and talk about just what might be going on inside and outside the world of Stephen Dedalus' mind. Such knowledge for the commentator need not be from inside Catholicism, but it should be profound and careful. In *Stephen Hero,* Stephen reflects that "the entire theory, in accordance with which his entire artistic life was shaped, arose most conveniently for his purpose out of the mass of Catholic theology" (205). From inside or from outside Catholicism, it is a mistake to talk about Joyce as an "inverted mystic" and to chart the artistic development of Stephen in *A Portrait* as though it proceeded (receded?) by way of a five-fold or even three-fold inversion of the mystic's way at prayer. Father Merton does not attempt to do this, but there are others now who do. Father Merton himself too well knows from actual practice the ways of both poetry and mysticism to take the one way for the other, even in reverse. Irish Catholicism as it works out in practice is not just a checkerboard of symbols that the Joycean commentator can play with according to an improvised game of ideas. The confessions of the artists turn on pivots different from those of the saints; spiritual conversion or elections to the religion of art are not the same as what most men understand by conversions to a life of grace. The missions of the artists are of a different order from those of priests. There are likenesses and analogues between the service of God and man at the altar and the service of man and God through art, but there are also major differences that Joyce himself appreciated. Joyce did not renounce the religion of Catholicism so as to take on the uneasy practice and burden of a culture-religion. Without clear Catholic insights into some of these major differences, a commentator on Joyce may sound much like a tone-deaf analyst of Mozart or a color-blind interpreter of Van Gogh.

From the early notebooks of James Joyce and other family papers (most of them until lately unedited) at Cornell University and elsewhere, it is clear that, save for slight variations in key, Stephen Dedalus speaks as an alter ego or early voice of

Joyce himself when he was a young man. These same papers as well as many already published raw materials manifest also how mistaken the reader would be to conclude from *A Portrait* that everything that happens here to Stephen in this fiction actually happened in this same way, or at all, to Joyce in real life. The artist is an imaginer, not just a chronicler. A former Dubliner who shared schooldays in Dublin with James and Stanislaus Joyce has written to me, April 14, 1958: "If James Joyce did any reading in Philosophy [at University College], it was extracurricular and just some of the desultory reading that all of us did in the National Library." This same correspondent speaks of the annual retreat at Belvedere College in a different vein from Stephen's version of such a retreat in Chapter III of *A Portrait:* "At Belvedere there was an Annual Retreat lasting three days. . . . Invariably, *one* of the discourses was on Hell, or the punishment due to sin. It was only one of the discourses, and certainly at the end of the Retreat, the impression left as a climax was that the Mercy of God was boundless, and that you had but to love Him here on earth and you would enjoy His love forever in Heaven." But, then, *this* correspondent went on himself to Canada to be a successful engineer, not East to the Continent to be a world-famous artist. Still, there are other consciences besides the artist's and other integrities than just the artistic.

This variation in reappraisal, through the haze of time, of a Belvedere College retreat is a fair example of the difference between the truths of fiction and of fact. Both are true! Both are not the same! Whether or not the retreat discourses by Father Arnall of *A Portrait* are ones that were actually preached to Joyce while he was still at Belvedere—by Father William Power, S.J., or by a Father Jeffcoate, S.J., or as appears to me more likely (if I had to choose) by Father James A. Cullen, S.J., the spiritual father at Belvedere, or by still another Jesuit— is for literature unimportant. Somebody preached this kind of retreat, to judge from Joyce's report of Stephen Dedalus' traumatic recollections in *A Portrait*. The effect of it was in the fiction to turn Stephen for a time from a life of sin to an aesthetic life untarnished. "He saw . . . . he wept for the innocence he had lost" (137, 139), "How simple and beautiful was life after all" (146).

For the sake of his fiction, Joyce shows this change of heart in Stephen as a conversion to the life beautiful. Stephen's subsequent trial by scruples shows how much the effort cost Stephen to treat this conversion as though it were to a life of supernatural grace. How understandable at the end is Stephen's refusal, "I will not serve" (239).

We know by now that the particular sermons that Stephen in *A Portrait* recollects are in fact closely modeled on Father Giovanni Pinamonti's *Hell Opened to Christians*. Father Pinamonti was a seventeenth-century Italian Jesuit. These discourses of his were easily available in translation and in pamphlet form to Joyce in Dublin, and were probably used by the retreat masters who went to Belvedere College. Joyce might have read them in Dublin near the time when he started writing *Stephen Hero*. He appears clearly to have read them before he finished *A Portrait* in Italy, at Trieste.[14] No matter. Joyce improves the rhetoric of Pinamonti, but Pinamonti is still Joyce's "original," not Father Cullen, nor whomever Father Arnall might in recalled fact represent.

So when one says that an artist needs to write from his personal experience, one needs also to add that the life of the books that an artist reads is part of that personal experience, *his* life of the mind. Joyce is a great borrower. For example, one poetical phrase from *A Portrait* that is usually assumed to be Joyce's own has been shown lately to be another of many borrowings: "A day of dappled seaborne clouds" (166). James S. Atherton, in his Notes to his (Heinemann) edition of *A Portrait*, points out that this phrase is a quotation from Hugh Miller's

The Testimony of the Rocks (Edinburgh, 1869, p. 237). Atherton notes also the many pervasive echoes of Newman that are orchestrated into Joyce's *Portrait* text. Stephen once tells a friend that he considers Newman to be "the greatest writer" of them all (80). Often he borrows phrases from Newman's sermon "The Glories of Mary," but he also often borrows from Newman's other works. As Atherton shows, most of these Newman quotations—all of them, it now seems—are extracted from a single collection called *Characteristics from the Writings of J. H. Newman,* ed. W. S. Lilly (London, 1875).

"But you could not have a green rose":—so, when he was a little boy, Stephen thought to himself one day in class at the Clongowes Wood school of *A Portrait* (7, 13). Joyce's imagination here is searching to find a way to make "the green rose" blossom for Stephen and for himself, "O, the wild rose blossoms," as he says here on his first page. So at the very start of this remembrance, a phrase from the song "Lilly Dale" announces the dominant theme of the composition as a whole. Even Stephen longs often to escape from "the cold silence of intellectual revolt" (181). "I'm a ballocks," not "Ireland's hope. . . . I am and I know I am,"—so even Stephen, now a young man, once tells his friends. "And I admit that I am" (231). That is one of Stephen's finest moments, and shows that Stephen does not take himself quite so seriously as some of Joyce's exegetes take him.

At the risk of appearing, oneself, to take Stephen's story too seriously, one might here, for the sake of completion, mention a possible submerged theme in this story, one to which almost no attention, so far as I know, has yet been paid. I refer to its homosexual undertone. Joyce is not explicit, Stephen appears to be unconscious that he is taking this tone, but I surmise that Joyce himself was conscious of the submerged homosexual material of *A Portrait.* He had used this kind of material already in his second *Dubliners* story, "An Encounter." In that short story, significantly, Joyce shows us a young boy, Mahony, an extrovert, not at all artistic, who has a prompt and healthy reaction to perversion; and Joyce shows another young boy, the boy-narrator, the artist, who is baffled by the mystery of perversion and who needs in panic at the end to call out to his extrovert friend for rescue: "And I was penitent; for in my heart I had always despised him a little." About the same time that he published *A Portrait,* Joyce used this kind of observation explicitly in his now published Notes, in his play, *Exiles* (1918).

Stephen Dedalus' voice speaking of his relations with girls (even in his "swoon of sin" with the prostitute, 101) conveys a strange tone, now of vagueness, now of hostility. It seems as though he does not know girls well or like them. His comments on men sound at times disturbed and disturbing. Stephen's recollections of his childhood friends, especially of Wells and of Simon Moonan, even of Mr. Gleeson (who, I suppose, is a Jesuit Scholastic), come through as though in Stephen's fantasy they were on the homosexual side. His relations with his parents, as they are here recollected, especially his many acts of sensitiveness, his hostilities to his mother and about her, appear almost at times as though they were written in a Freudian code. Freud's scientific analyses of human behavior were not Joyce's cup of tea. But Freud was much in the air in the early 1900's, his preconscious was being much talked about, and Joyce had access to all these Freudian theories in German itself, or, if he wished by 1916, in English translation. Freud was being discussed all over Europe by 1916. As an artist, Joyce did not need to commit himself to Freudianism— any more so than he needed to commit himself to Thomism. He committed himself to neither, but where it pleased him he used both as literary materials, the moralism of Saint Thomas (more so than Saint Thomas's slight, incidental aesthetics) and the psychoanalytic theories of Freud.

In Stephen's more cerebral moods a repressed aggressiveness appears, which might account for his adolescent disenchantment with "Mother" Church, or, for that matter, with a Father Church, or with any Church at all. Dogmatic, or doctrinal, impossibilities for those who cannot accept them, that is, longer abide by them, are more often than not rooted in moral difficulties. Cranly once tells Stephen, "your mind is supersaturated with the religion in which you say you disbelieve" (240). A little later Stephen answers Cranly, "I said that I had lost the faith, . . . but not that I had lost selfrespect" (243-244). Stephen goes away from Catholicism without visible hysteria, but Joyce here shows a mind much troubled: "And I am not afraid to make a mistake, even a great mistake, a life-long mistake and perhaps as long as eternity too" (247). And Stephen goes away from Ireland alone. *He* does not take a radiant Nora with him.

So far as a homosexual syndrome is here imagined, Joyce's materials in *A Portrait* are veiled. Such a syndrome is not, to be sure, the whole story but it sounds in *A Portrait* like part of it. Stephen's homosexual memories are presented as fantasies, a war within more than without. Joyce does not represent them, it is true, as metaphysical abstractions of cosmic worth. A reader, nevertheless, is sometimes led to wonder about the odd emphases given by Joyce to some of Stephen's graphic details: "Such was a queer word" (11), the much whispered-about homosexual scandal that involves Simon Moonan while Stephen is still a small boy at Clongowes Wood (11).[15] At Belvedere College, Stephen once notices "a stout old lady" kneeling at the altar "in a dark corner of the chapel at the gospel side," and beside her is her son, Bertie Tallon, who is dressed in pink and "wearing a curly golden wig" (74). The "original" for this "pink dressed figure" was a boy at Belvedere named Bertie

A Portrait: After Fifty Years 79

Sheridan, who performed a solo dance, "The sunbonnet dance," in a play, *Vice Versa,* in which Joyce himself actually performed. There actually were rough and ready boys then at Belvedere who were named Tallon; here Joyce transfers the family name of this rough, tough lot of boys to the effeminate figure. At University College, Stephen has odd impressions of Cranly at times, mysterious, dark, here inexplicable: "a guilty priest" (178), "Cranly's dark eyes were watching him" (194).

Homosexual fantasies are not abnormal in childhood; at least, they are not uncommon. Nor are they uncommon even in adolescent friendships. Stephen's later kind of heterosexual bravado, even ruthlessness, is also not an uncommon later kind of reaction. Such a young man often discovers in himself a quality that he does not like. Whether this is a neurosis or a simple physical inclination, he may try with vengeance to eradicate it or reverse it. So, anyway, Joyce here arranges his verbal score. He orchestrates the dissonance; he does not, as some might today, play it as a dominant leitmotif. Stephen's adolescent fantasies are here much refined by Joyce's older, more experienced mind.

The presence of so many priests, most of them Jesuits, Stephen's educators, [also Joyce's] obliges readers of *A Portrait* to decide whether their being here is good or bad. Kevin Sullivan, in *Joyce among the Jesuits,* has gone into this question more thoroughly than has anyone else, and his report is mixed.[16] Stephen's own report in *A Portrait* is on the whole benign: for example, "Whatever he had heard or read of the craft of jesuits he had put aside frankly as not borne out by his own experience. His masters, even when they had not attracted him, had seemed to him always intelligent and serious priests" (155-156). Stephen recalls his traumatic experience with the cruel prefect of studies at Clongowes, Father Dolan, but he also recalls afterwards the kindness to him of his own teacher, Father Arnall:

"His voice was very gentle and soft. . . . And Father Arnall had said that he need not study till the new glasses came" (51-52).

In some ways, certainly, these Irish Jesuits at the turn of the century failed Stephen, and their "originals," it seems, failed Joyce in his aspirations to be an artist. It appears that they were not so intelligent as they should have been. Not all of them were so gentle and holy as the ideals of their priestly vocations obliged. It is not difficult to understand why such an earnest young artist as Stephen (or, for that matter, Joyce) should be unhinged by some kinds of example and counsel that were given. These Jesuits might, it seems, have opened their own minds and hearts more generously to what was going on in this young artist's creative heart and mind: so at least *A Portrait* shows.

The reader of *A Portrait* notices, as Joyce wants him imaginatively to notice, some of the awful stupidities and silences of these former priest-mentors of Stephen. Joyce also assumes, expects his readers to assume, that genius, religious or artistic, is almost never properly understood and rightly dealt with by the genius's own living mentors and peers. Being misunderstood and mishandled are included in the usual cost that any artist pays for his art. Sometimes too a built-in flaw in personality is also included in the high price that an artist needs to pay in personal cost for excellence. Achievement seldom comes cheap.

Some of Joyce's commentators tend to blur the distinction between his achievement in art and the success-failure of his religious life of supernatural faith. Joyce for himself saw the difference. Faith in art is grounded on the grace of art; no one just manufactures serious art. Religious faith is grounded on another kind of grace. Joyce's close friend Jacques Mercanton has told us, "Although a connoisseur of blasphemies, he remained always within the most orthodox frame of reference, his mind curiously closed to every form of heresy, in the moral as in the religious order." When Mercanton goes on to call *Finnegans Wake* "a work of reconciliation," he adds, "not in the sense of a return to the Church, still less in a kind of spiritual substitution, a function that might conceivably be assigned to poetry. One cannot replace the Christian faith, and there is no mask for the face of Christ. Besides nothing could be more alien to Joyce's spirit."[17]

For all that he represented of the faults and failures of these Irish Jesuit educators of his, Joyce understood better, far, than most of his commentators how much he owed to the Jesuits. More than once he expressed his admiration and gratitude. The conclusions could be appalling were one wryly to wonder how his life of the mind might for fourteen years have unfolded in some English public schools of his time, or in some less discriminating American public schools and state universities of our time. In *Life and the Dream,* Mary Colum speaks of Joyce as "the most outstanding advertisement in literature" for the sort of education that he—she as well—received at University College, Dublin.[18]

"I was telling the things I couldn't frame in words. I was singing the story of my misery and confusion, of the misunderstandings in my life I couldn't straighten out, the story of the wrongs and outrages done to me by people I had loved and trusted. Your imagination can carry you just so far. Only those who have been hurt deeply can understand what pain is, or humiliation. Only those who are being burned know what fire is like."

This last quotation of mine is not from *A Portrait* of Joyce, but from the autobiography (probably ghost-written) of another superb artist. It is Ethel Waters telling us how she felt as she interpreted her song "Stormy Weather" on the Cotton Club floor.[19] Joyce at the end, in *Finnegans Wake,* calls the literary artist a "shemshamsshowman" (530). The earlier quasi-autobiography, *A Portrait,* is a stormy story, sad-glad and troubled and defiant, as the stories of young people who are artists almost always are. Joyce's imagination is vitally at work as he tries to frame his own story in words. As he says in his epigraph from Ovid at the start of this story, "he devoted his mind to unknown arts." But, then: "Your imagination can carry you just so far."

5

THE POSITION OF *ULYSSES* TODAY

Richard M. Kain

Joyce followed the early career of *Ulysses* with the naive pride of a Stephen Hero and the business acumen of a Leopold Bloom. In his letters he releases publicity, reports orders (from the British Museum and the *Times*), and awaits reviews impatiently. He greets Arnold Bennett's favorable critique with the shrewd comment that "For the purpose of sales his article is not very useful as it does not give the name and address of the publisher." He suggests sending copies of the *Observer,* "marked with red pencil," to Quinn, Linati, and Benco: "The day after the article appeared 145 letters came asking for prospectuses." He makes an addition to the leaflet of press notices being prepared by Harriet Weaver, and plants a letter "for Miss Beach to send to the critic of the *Quarterly"* regarding the number of press copies. The letter concludes "with a brief mention of the second edition." Joyce adds, with apologetic self-mockery, "I am sure all this will seem very disingenuous to you but alas you must speak Helvetian to a Swiss."

Joyce could speak Helvetian. He planned his own publicity strategy like a generalissimo, rushing in reinforcements where necessary and husbanding such reserves as the scheme of *Ulysses,* which he allowed certain friends to see but which was not to be printed, until it appeared in Stuart Gilbert's study (1930).

His interest never flagged, through seizures, piracies, translations, university lectures, plans for filming, and critiques. In 1932 he wrote to Frank Budgen that "Nine persons seem to be engaged in doing books about me at present." A year later he reported to Budgen that Louis Gillet "wants a chair in *Me* to be founded at Geneva where he can be my commentator."

There is no doubt that Joyce would delight in the acclaim he still commands. He would note the number of items—1434—in Robert H. Deming's bibliography, and would undoubtedly be the first to make additions. Though Geneva never established a Joyce chair for Gillet, the number of Joyce courses and seminars, especially in the United States, is now beyond count. Books, notes, and reviews have recently averaged about 275 a year. American doctoral theses began modestly (one in 1944, two in 1948) but the tide soon rose (twenty-four in the fifties, twenty in 1960-1963).

All this annotation, explication, and interpretation raises two crucial questions. Can *Ulysses* (and the other works) survive this heavy freight, and if so, what does it contribute to our understanding? Ithaca may at last be within sight, but Homer's myth may be re-enacted, with the craft sinking just off shore.

Detailed discussion of Joyceana—even of "Ulysseana"—is obviously out of the question here. The only feasible procedure is to survey the main areas of study, with the admonition that the necessary brevity of comment may lead to an unintended tone of dogmatic assurance.

I *The Genesis of* Ulysses

Discovering an author's creative process, one of the most puzzling of literary problems, must in the case of Joyce's *Ulysses* be deduced retrospectively through what we know of the gestation of *Finnegans Wake,* or by anticipation, that is, by extrapolation from Joyce's early work. Neither procedure is reliable, of course, and each must be handled with circumspection. In the case of *Finnegans Wake* we must pre-date attitudes by some ten years or more, and attribute to the author opinions which evolved under circumstances of another quite different work. Post-dating the views of youth involves a further complication, that of distinguishing between the actual and the fictional, separating the successive Stephens of the "Portrait" essay, of *Stephen Hero,* of *A Portrait of the Artist,* and of *Ulysses,* from the successive James Joyces of 1904 to 1921, who created them. Nonetheless a fairly consistent pattern does seem to emerge. We can trace a steadily increasing preoccupation with the symbolic, or rather the sacramental, view of existence. The term "sacramental" seems preferable for its religious overtones, and for its avoidance of the implication that Joyce's method was one of mechanical "symbol insertion." The word "sacramental" also tends to warn undiscriminating readers who view with awe each trivial item in the text. Joyce, to be sure, did relish what might seem idle coincidences, and the suggested change in terminology is no guarantee of a sound critical method. Nevertheless it appears that we may be on the threshold of distinguishing which motifs are more significant and fruitful. But these speculations soon lead to matters of interpretation.

II *Textual Development*

Joyce's mode of writing by accretion makes this editorial task basic. The *Finnegans Wake* materials, both notebooks and rough drafts, are much more extensive than those for *Ulysses,* yet the earlier work has significant textual data, as indicated by the studies of Joseph Prescott in the essays collected as *Exploring James Joyce* (1964). The expectation is that a textual variorum might lead to new perspectives of insight. No clue is more valuable. From manuscript to final page proof, additions were made in the interest of precision, specification, tonal appropriateness, and euphony. To select only a few examples, Stephen Dedalus "watched through quivering peacock lashes the southing sun." The central phrase then became, successively, "peacockquivering," "peacocktwinkling," and finally "peacocktwittering." An afterthought with humorous effect is found in late galleys, where the Plumtree label is followed first by the statement, "Beware of imitation," then in final proofs by examples of anagrammatic variation: "Peatmot. Trumplee. Montpat. Plamtroo." Joyce's skill in rhythmic imitation is well illustrated by his improvements and additions to a description of the viceregal cavalcade. First, "A cavalcade in easy trot along Pembroke quay passed, outriders leaping gracefully in their saddles." The final version has the "outriders leaping, leaping in their, in their saddles," echoed several pages later by the sentence, "In saddles of the leaders, leaping leaders, rode outriders."

III *The Text*

It is unfortunate that the standard American edition was set up from a faulty text, and that its revision, though many errors were corrected, is still far from perfect. Equally frustrating is the failure to follow the pagination of its predecessor, thus rendering incorrect all references in basic studies from 1937 to 1962 or thereabouts. One might hope that before long a corrected text will be published, preferably with annotations and, as suggested above, with variant readings from proof and the *Little Review* text.

Two recent doctoral theses, available in University Microfilms, suggest the inadequacy of present texts. Norman Silverstein's "Joyce's Circe Episode . . ." (Columbia University, 1960) lists about 130 errata in the earlier Random House edition, only about one-third of which were corrected in the revision of 1961. Robert E. Hurley lists twenty errata in the 1961 version of the third chapter ("The Proteus Episode of James Joyce's *Ulysses,*" Columbia, 1963). An indication of the wanderings of the *Ulysses* text is given by the extant sources for "Circe," as listed by Silverstein: manuscripts and typescripts at Buffalo, at the Rosenbach Foundation Museum in Philadelphia, and, one page, at Southern Illinois University; page proofs at Harvard, Buffalo, and Texas. To make the subject international as well, we must add the excellent corrected text from the Odyssey Press in Hamburg, and the French translation, supervised by Joyce (Paris, 1928).

IV *Exegesis*

The epic quality of *Ulysses* derives largely from its richness of reference. The Dublin ethos provided a fertile loam for Joyce's imagination, and it is regrettable that no Dubliner of Joyce's generation took the book seriously enough to provide more than casual identifications. To the educated Irishman the book was at best a kind of local joke book, or an elaborate hoax. Without doubt many allusions to the Irish scene must remain hidden.

Another factor in regard to the ephemeral allusion was convincingly demonstrated by Robert M. Adams in *Surface and Symbol* (1962). Adams showed that, far from being the perfect work of art and artifice which its admirers claimed, *Ulysses* is a flawed masterpiece containing a detritus of error, irrelevance, and personal animosity. Judging from the extensive detective work Mr. Adams engaged in, the final reading of *Ulysses* would constitute an overwhelming task of exhumation. Short of that, we can cull from the reminiscences of Gogarty, Sheehy, Stanislaus Joyce, and other memorialists many details of place and personality which constitute the ambience of Joyce's Dublin.

Of almost equal difficulty is the task of tracking down literary and historical allusions, since Joyce's source materials were seldom conventional. These references, too, are often distorted deliberately for comic or associational effects, or submerged in the flow of consciousness. We are getting on with the job, however, as may be seen in the series of annotations by Weldon Thornton which have appeared in the *James Joyce Quarterly*.

The purposes of these allusions are often obscure. *Ulysses* is written in a distinctive mode where levels of usage and meaning converge or strain in polar tension. The result is that the book is about a city and a civilization and is itself an artifact of that city and civilization. No other fiction, excepting *Finnegans Wake* and *Tristram Shandy,* calls attention so insistently to the fact that it is a work of verbal artifice, of contrived structure and style. The author's use of colored pencils in his manuscripts suggested to Valery Larbaud the analogy of mosaic. If a mosaic, *Ulysses* can better be seen as following the principles of abstract expressionism rather than those of Byzantine stylization.

V *Thematics*

A subsidiary form of explication is the analytical study of important themes. One of the hallmarks of a major literary work is the degree to which such study of isolated topics is fruitful. On this level the magnitude of Shakespeare or Milton or Tolstoy is apparent, for each absorbed within his work so many vital contemporary currents of thought and feeling that it is only a slight exaggeration to use terms such as "the age of Shakespeare."

Thematic analysis is less popular in English and American than in French criticism, judging from the variety of book-length special studies of Marcel Proust. Shakespeare, Aquinas, vocal music, and the Church Fathers are the only topics treated thus far at book length by Joyce scholars. Handled with the proper insight and tact, analysis of other themes might be desirable. Joyce's command of language has been more often asserted than demonstrated. His awareness of levels of style and problems of communication makes *Ulysses* a true Rosetta Stone of modern culture, from the level of mass advertising to that of political oratory. It may be predicted with some confidence that *Ulysses* will retain for considerable time its hold on the contemporary imagination, and that this centrality will be reflected in more thorough and more subtle scholarly analyses.

VI *Interpretation*

In *Ulysses* complexity of allusion is paralleled by diversity of tone, and Joyce can be held just as responsible for the latitude of interpretation as for the mass of exegesis. Within limits, variety implies vitality, but what, one may ask, are the requisite limits? Though some would argue for an unlimited range of interpretation and others would hold that no limits be sought outside of the work itself, it would seem that if the study of literature be a responsible expression of the human spirit all available evidence should be utilized.

It appears that most of the extant evidence is now available. Joyce's marginal creative work has been collected and published, most notably *Stephen Hero,* the Epiphanies, the 1904 essay "A Portrait of the Artist," the *Exiles* Notes, and the miscellaneous critical writings. And it is doubtful whether much important biographical information remains undiscovered. Only in the case of the letters will considerable additional data be forthcoming.

The professional study of *Ulysses* in recent years has disposed of some of the more extreme views widely held when the book first appeared. No one now would responsibly consider it a hoax, or the product of a madman's delusions. A book so patiently elaborated over many years must be accepted as a serious work of art. Its stature is established beyond doubt; in fact, it runs the risk of becoming institutionalized as a modern classic.

A new generation, having missed the drama of disputation which accompanied the defense of *Ulysses* after World War I, is in danger of settling down into its own orthodoxy. Joyce's emancipating force is not only denied but reversed, and we are offered a Joyce more Catholic than the Catholics. Such interpreters forget many of the author's explicit statements, such as his confession to Nora during his courtship in 1904, that he had left the Church six years before, "hating it most fervently." No longer would he wage the "secret war" of his student days: "Now I make open war upon it by what I write and say and do." It might be argued that this letter, printed in full by Ellmann, is yet another gesture of revolt, like his concurrent socialistic phase. One could find confirmation of Joyce's delight in self-dramatization in the obviously Byronic role he created for himself, and his disarming admission a bit later in the same letter: "I cannot enter the social order except as a vagabond," he asserts, and then, apologizing for some extreme statement he had made during the evening, "Can you not see the simplicity which is at the back of all my disguises?" "We all wear masks," he continued, adopting the image from Wilde which was to prove so useful to Yeats. According to his brother Stanislaus, Joyce did claim kinship for his art with "the mystery of the Mass" in the sense of "converting the bread of everyday life into something that has a permanent artistic life of its own." More pertinent is his predilection for the symbolic mode, in which critics will continue to see evidence of Catholic rearing. The most plausible interpretation will probably not go much further than to regard the mature Joyce as at best a "sympathetic alien," to adopt the title of J. Mitchell Morse's study.

If Joyce now appears more a Catholic than formerly, he is

also more a Dubliner. Early critics emphasized the "Wasteland" aspects of *Ulysses,* following Ezra Pound's essay on the resemblance of *Ulysses* to Flaubert's desolating anti-bourgeois satire *Bouvard and Pécuchet.* Appearing in the *Mercure de France* in June 1922, it was the second important review-essay, the first being Valery Larbaud's study which had appeared two months before in the *Nouvelle Revue Française.* Herbert Gorman's biography was a portrait of a gloomy exile from a city described as "A place for the dying, perhaps, where the leaping thought was speedily caged," and as "a small, bickering, treacherous world which did not desire him (the arrogant non-conformist) any more than he desired it." Gorman's highly colored view has been attributed to his American-Irish embarrassment for his own background, but Richard Ellmann has recently shown that Joyce's own last-minute emendations themselves were sufficient (Ellmann's words) "to curb a sporadic cheeriness in Gorman's book, and to render more solemn and sardonic its picture of the persecuted artist."

Ulysses was written at a relatively happy time in respect to the author's attitude toward his native city. The bitterness of early revolt had passed, and disappointment at lack of recognition there was yet to come. Dublin stood in the middle distance, and could be recollected with nostalgia and with an almost mellow humor.

Admirers of *Ulysses* have usually resented the implication of scatology, and have defended the author's frankness on grounds of honesty to the physiological facts of life, or as a symptom of moral revulsion. They have smiled knowingly at Nora Joyce's remarks about her husband's "dirty mind." The fact of the matter seems to be that the trait was not limited to Joyce himself, for Nora had it equally, judging from the atsonishingly outspoken correspondence between them in 1909. An informed and sympathetic study of this correspondence (which is now at Cornell) is that of Mary T. Reynolds in the *Sewanee Review*

(Winter, 1964), "Joyce and Nora: The Indispensable Countersign." According to this interpretation their mutual erotic experience was their only dependable bond:

> In no other aspect of their relationship was there so much basic confidence and harmony. . . . As the details of their intimate life are set forth it becomes apparent that issues between them which could not be resolved on any rational basis of argument or persuasion could be and were cleared away by inviting and receiving the emotional response of one personality to the other.

Indeed, the union, at least in its early years, seems to have been a sad story of anxiety, frustration, and incompatibility, relieved only by extreme eroticism.

Critics and scholars have been understandably reluctant to accept psychological and psycho-analytic approaches to literature, fearing that the creative impulse be reduced to the level of a symptom, a rudimentary mechanism of compensation or sublimation. The whole truth must be admitted, regardless. Joyce shared with many Irishmen a prurient curiosity which has been attributed to the Jansenist repressiveness of the national moral climate. In addition he was oddly prudish in conversation. However we interpret this complex of responses, we may anticipate that the author's lack of reticence need no longer disturb the reader of *Ulysses*. The level of public acceptance has changed so markedly within the generation that the outspokenness of *Ulysses* no longer provokes comment. Indeed, once it has been admitted, the manifold other aspects of the novel can receive proper attention.

VII *The Symbolistic Mode*

Joyce was ambivalent regarding the circulation of his chart of correspondences, perhaps sensing the danger of appearing a mechanical craftsman. When a scheme was first published and

The Position of *Ulysses* Today

discussed by Stuart Gilbert in 1930—there are in fact several variants—it did give rise to a widespread suspicion of perverse and misplaced ingenuity. At this time the earliest published bits of *Work in Progress* were at hand for confirmation. It might almost be said that knowledge of the author's blueprint detracted somewhat from the considerable enthusiasm that *Ulysses* first aroused among its admirers.

Since no rationale for the method was provided, it seemed reasonable to ignore the arcana of organs, colors, arts, symbols, and techniques, and to think of the chart as a scaffold which had little relevance to the finished work. The French *symbolistes* were not well-known at the time, though essays by Arthur Symons *(The Symbolist Movement in Literature)* and W. B. Yeats *(Ideas of Good and Evil)* had long been available. Thanks to the concern of the New Criticism with the nature of poetic knowledge and the significance of poetic language, together with exegesis of modern and metaphysical poetry, notably of Yeat's later poems and his esoteric system, expounded in *A Vision,* together with the slow emergence of a reading of *Finnegans Wake,* this final handicap has gradually been overcome.

Once more the availability of biographical data and ephemeral writing has revealed the consistency of the author's insight. From the time he altered and added details to his first published story, "The Sisters", that is, about 1905, to his late reflections as recorded by Jacques Mercanton, Joyce was seeking to read the "signatures" of objects, myths, themes, etymologies. Mercanton recalls his curiosity about the names of places, of mountains, of wines at Lausanne: "He repeated the words, came back to them, compared them, toyed with their sounds, their assonances, his mind constantly active." This evocative memoir contains other glimpses of his care for phonetic precision. He corrected an expression about a friend's mental illness, "I foresaw it," to the more accurate, "I was afraid it might happen." Seeing soccer players, he asked about the French names for the positions. He claimed that his linguistic distortions in the *Wake* followed historical precedents. Always restlessly curious, he put everything he knew, everything he remembered, into his two great works. Fate and accident were on his side. Homeric and other literary parallels, symbols, liturgical echoes, all became relevant to the giant epiphanies, which, it may be concluded, will thus never be completely read.

VIII *Retrospect and Prospect*

The commentary continues to appear, its annual volume probably approximating that of Joyce's complete works. And no wonder, for if a detailed exegesis of *Finnegans Wake* would require many volumes, *Ulysses* would need only slightly fewer.

The most complete bibliography of Joyce studies is Robert Deming's, which covers publications through early 1962. Any listing or assessment is almost immediately obsolete. A perceptive appraisal of the literature about Joyce is given by Harry Levin in the second edition (1960) of his *James Joyce,* a book which from its first appearance in 1941 has held undisputed priority as a basic study. An extensive account of the early reception of *Ulysses* and the principal types of interpretation is found in *Joyce, The Man, The Work, The Reputation* (1956), by Marvin Magalaner and the present writer. Current American books and articles are listed in the annual bibliographical issues of *Publications of the Modern Language Association*. Two Joyce journals are presently being published, the *James Joyce Quarterly* (Tulsa, Oklahoma) and *The Wake Newslitter* (Newcastle, New South Wales).

The most pressing need today is for a corrected text, preferably retaining the earlier pagination. Highly desirable is a variorum of notes and of textual variants in the manuscripts. The problem of detailing with the mass of interpretation is more difficult. A bibliography raisonée, with fairly extensive summary and quotation, will shortly become a necessity.

Frank Kermode has asserted that the reputation of *Ulysses* in England has declined. In *Puzzles and Epiphanies* (1962) he reprinted a 1959 review-article which stated that "The power of *Ulysses* to possess a man's mind seems to have flagged." "Under thirty, people seem to be a little bored by Joyce's endless experimentation" and the younger generation "are not much interested in the vast ambition . . . to make of a book an entire self-supporting world, a reality which, like normal reality, is a paradigm of some inaccessible truth."

Robert Martin Adams reaches similar conclusions regarding Joyce's American reputation. He finds "Joyce in the Sixties" (*Partisan Review,* Fall 1962) "not by any means the same force he was in the twenties," for "the things he was able to hang people up on in the twenties—like the theory of epiphany, the bit about Dedalus the maze-maker, and the great Earth-mother image—are starting to look a little threadbare." So too, the elaborate symbolistic scaffolding, which has not proven rewarding to readers, nor useful to current novelists. These are serious assessments, coming as they do from balanced and wise critics. To what degree they are applicable, in England or elsewhere, it is difficult to say. One who has a vested professional interest, like the present writer, is not a good judge. It may be a peculiar American mania, this Joyce industry that the English so often deride; at any rate it is a fact that in American academic circles at least, *Ulysses* continues to absorb the attention of critics and scholars.

6

JAMES JOYCE IN THE SMITHY OF HIS SOUL

William Blissett

I

"Welcome, O life! I go to encounter for the millionth time the reality of experience and to forge in the smithy of my soul the uncreated conscience of my race." Climactic and penultimate words. Stephen Dedalus has seen into the labyrinth of his vocation; more, he turns his gaze at last away from his own proper person to invoke a paternal spirit: "Old father, old artificer, stand me now and ever in good stead."[1]

The intermittently puzzling, occasionally irradiating thought of his legendary father touches and quickens but does not form or comprise Stephen's inmost self, and the association of himself with Icarus (as elsewhere with Byron or with Lucifer) cannot be taken as an identification, for Icarus borrowed his father's gear and failed, whereas Stephen resolves to forge his own and succeeds. Some other image, allusion, mythical identification, must be present with power to guide his mind—a figure that encounters reality with a new and self-forged weapon. The figure's name is withheld, but an effort of investigation will disclose it.

When Stephen as a boy was reading *The Count of Monte Cristo,* he first felt that a special vocation was reserved and would be revealed to him. "He wanted to meet in the real world the unsubstantial image which his soul so constantly beheld. He did not know where to seek it or how, but a premonition which led him on told him that this image would, without any overt act of his, encounter him."[2] The key word is "encounter." Here the boy passively imagines a woman of grace, an ALP, just as the boy in "An Encounter" passively meets a man of sin, an HCE. Clearly these two and our epigraph are companion passages, separated by the years of adolescence, by a modulation from passive to active, from the third to the first person. The modulation is all in the score of the novel.

The integrity of childhood splits into the riot and inward division of adolescence. "Nothing moved him or spoke to him from the real world unless he heard in it an echo of the infuriated cries within him." This tension issues into a reflexive "going-forth" but not an active "encounter"; "It was his own soul going forth to experience, unfolding itself sin by sin, spreading abroad the bale-fire of its burning stars and folding back upon itself, fading slowly, quenching its own lights and fires." And after this first going forth comes the first recoil, the countermovement of repentance, which is three times associated with a sword or spear, a weapon not forged or wielded by himself. Shining "through the fissure between the last blind and the sash a shaft of wan light entered like a spear"; Stephen sees this in the chapel, and after the sermon, "the thought slid like a cold shining rapier into his tender flesh: confession." "Cowering in darkness and abject, he prayed mutely to his angel guardian to drive away with his sword the demon that was whispering to his brain." The prayer is answered, but still at the cost of "encounter," for in his new state "the world for all its solid substance and complexity no longer existed for his soul save as a theorem of divine power and love and universality." Was it for this that his blood murmured "like a sinful city summoned from its sleep to hear its doom"? Grave and blind in servitude, is Stephen never to read the book of himself?[3]

Quietly, however, he is maturing. Some of the judgments of his superiors begin to sound a little childish to him, arousing a certain regret or pity, "as though he were slowly passing out of an accustomed world and were hearing its language for the last time." Not again is priestly power associated with a punishing or a restraining sword; Stephen stands free to go. He does not move at once. No longer cowering and abject, his imagination detains him, "accomplishing the vague acts of the priesthood which pleased him by reason of their semblance of reality and of their distance from it. . . . In vague sacrificial or sacramental acts alone his will seemed drawn to go forth to encounter reality." Now it is, while he is drawn to "secret knowledge and secret power," that the name of "the fabulous artificer," "the hawklike man," becomes for him a "prophecy of the end he had been born to serve," giving him courage to say to the other discipline *"non serviam"*. Daedalus becomes for him "a symbol of the artist forging anew in his workshop out of the sluggish matter of the earth a new soaring impalpable imperishable being."[4]

The composite figure of Daedalus-Icarus seems now to have taken full possession of Stephen. "An instant of wild flight had delivered him and the cry of triumph which his lips withheld cleft his brain." But what is this cry that cleaves the anvil of his brain, so that he feels "his cheeks aflame and his throat throbbing with song"? Why it is that "a new wild life was singing in his veins," that "he was unheeded, happy, and near to the wild heart of life"?[5] The answer is not made explicit until late in *Ulysses*. He goes on now to reiterate the Daedalian images of flight and artifice, to think of himself as risen from the grave of boyhood and to recall again the promise of free and powerful creation.

After this heightened passage comes the subdued discussion with the dean, which begins with the priest saying "There is an art in lighting a fire," and Stephen replying, "I will try to learn it." If the one is also thinking about the fire of the altar, the other is thinking of his forge in which (to anticipate somewhat) he would be "a priest of eternal imagination, transmuting the daily bread of experience into the radiant body of everlasting life." It should be observed that the note of ironic misgiving—a signal to the reader to begin the long process of dissociating himself from Stephen Dedalus—occurs in this phase of the book and in connection with the same image of the smithy. "Yet it wounded him to think that he would never be but a shy guest at the feast of the world's culture and that the monkish learning, in terms of which he was striving to forge out an aesthetic philosophy, was held no higher by the age he lived in than the subtle and curious jargons of heraldry and falconry." The swoon of sin and the swoon of prayer have given way to a swoon of art with (as it befell) *Finnegans Wake* far in the distance: "His soul was swooning into some new world, fantastic, dim, uncertain as under sea, traversed by cloudy shapes and beings." This state of weariness and agitation is given a prop in Stephen's ashplant, his mock-heroic, mock-priestly sword or wand. "The colonnade above him made him think vaguely of an ancient temple and the ashplant on which he leaned wearily of the curved stick of an augur. A sense of fear of the unknown moved in the heart of his weariness, a fear of symbols and portents, of the hawklike man whose name he bore soaring out of his captivity on osierwoven wings . . ."[6]

He beats "the frayed end of his ashplant against the base of a pillar"; later it is snatched from him and returned by Cranly; and at that point the bird call from *Siegfried* is whistled by Dixon. This occurs at the opening of Stephen's talk with Cranly in which he resolves on "silence, exile, and cunning," and at the end of the third-person narrative of the book. Add to these details the final entries in Stephen's diary with which we began, and one word from *Ulysses,* and the pieces are all present. The word is "Nothung!" the cry of triumph, the song of freedom, that the young Siegfried utters when he breaks the anvil with the reforged sword of his father Siegmund; it is the cry of triumph that Stephen utters as he brandishes his ashplant sword to break a glass chimney in Bella Cohen's brothel.[7]

Nothung, "Needful," Siegmund's sword, is what this young Siegfried has been trying to forge on the anvil of his brain, in the smithy of his soul. He has been learning (to move from Wagner to the first Wagnerite) how to go "Beyond Good and Evil, or How to Philosophize with a Hammer"; and, if he succeeds, he will be, like Wagner's young hero and like the hero of the mind that Nietzsche conceived as his model, "purely human" —fearless and free and without ties in the world he goes forth to encounter. The weary ashplant is at once the symbol of his failure and the symbol of his hope (or, to put it another way, it belongs equally to the realistic and the symbolist aspects of the two novels), and the breaking of the little light is both heroic climax and comic anticlimax of an action in which reality at last is encountered and a conscience forged for the most belated race in Europe. The Daedalus-Icarus image is forced into the open by Stephen's name, but the Siegfried image, though largely latent, is of equal strength in the context of the book and of far greater in the context of Joyce's world of ideas.

A Portrait of the Artist as a Young Man was written between 1904 and 1914. We know from his brother's memoirs that Joyce read "everything that Yeats had written in verse or prose." In August, 1907, W. B. Yeats wrote his essay of "Poetry and Patriotism," to be published the following year together with other papers by himself and Lionel Johnson in a book called *Poetry and Ireland*. Divagating at large on Irish patriotism and Irish country spiritism, and on Carlyle and Ruskin and Morris, Yeats, before expressing a disillusionment with societies and movements (doubtless congenial to such as Stephen who "were to be elusive of social or religious orders"), wrote this:

> A new belief seemed coming that would be so simple & demonstrable, and above all so mixed into the common scenery of the world, that it would set the whole man on fire and liberate

him from a thousand obediences and complexities. We were to forge in Ireland a new sword on our old traditional anvil for that great battle that must in the end re-establish the old confident joyous world.

In this heroic light (or twilight, or crépuscule, or Dämmerung) one may see Stephen's gesture as climax of the action shared by the *Portrait* and *Ulysses*.

The sword is all-but-identified as Siegfried's, and within a few pages Yeats goes on to mention Tristan and to speak of "the freedom of self-delight," a phrase supremely applicable to the young Siegfried. And further, Stephen's swoon into a weariness that works counter to the joy and confidence he aspires to: that too is adumbrated by Yeats, who concludes thus, "We artists, who are the servants not of any cause but of mere naked life, and above all of that life in its nobler forms, where joy and sorrow are one, Artificers of the Great Moment, became as elsewhere in Europe protesting individual voices."[8]

Round the writers and writings of the Irish literary Renaissance is a penumbra or fogbank of talk as big as Dublin, and we know from many sources how pervasive was the Wagnerism of the persons and movements concerned—Martyn and Moore, Symons and Miss Horniman, the Abbey Theatre and Theosophy. But among these George Moore stands in a very special relation to James Joyce, his *Untilled Field* being an earlier and rural forerunner of *Dubliners* and his *Confessions of a Young Man* being in title and substance a type and shadow of the *Portrait*. Moore wore his Wagnerism like a rash, and in 1914, the year of the *Portrait* and of the inception of *Ulysses,* he wrote in the concluding volume of his ironically vainglorious autobiography this passage,[9] which bears much the same relation to the mock-heroic element in Joyce as Yeats had done to the serious:

'She [Nature] intended to redeem Ireland from Catholicism and has chosen me as her instrument, and has cast chastity upon me so that I may be able to do her work,' I said. As soon as my change of life becomes known the women of Ireland will come to me crying, 'Master, speak to us, for, at the bidding of our magicians, we have borne children long enough. May we escape from the burden of child-bearing without sin?' they will ask me, and I will answer them: 'Ireland has lain too long under the spell of the magicians, without will, without intellect, useless and shameful, the despised of nations. I have come into the most impersonal country in the world to preach personality —personal love and personal religion, personal art, personality for all except for God'; and I walked across the greensward afraid to leave the garden, and to heighten my inspiration I looked toward the old apple tree, remembering that many had striven to draw forth the sword that Wotan had struck into the tree about which Hunding had built his hut. Parnell, like Sigmund, had drawn it forth, but Wotan had allowed Hunding to strike him with his spear. And the allegory becoming clearer I asked myself if I were Siegfried, son of Sigmund slain by Hunding, and if it were my fate to reforge the sword that lay broken in halves in Mimi's cave.

It seemed to me that the garden filled with tremendous music, out of which came a phrase glittering like a sword suddenly drawn from its sheath and raised defiantly to the sun.

It is as if the hero raised his ashplant to proclaim the new Bloomoosalem and to bring the blessings of contraception to Irish womanhood. This is the mock-heroic, the comic light by which Stephen's gesture is to be seen as an anticlimax and the true hero of *Ulysses* recognized as Leopold Bloom.

II

I have tried to indicate the depth and centrality of the identification of Stephen with Siegfried in the *Portrait* and *Ulysses*.

Further analysis will require as context some facts and deductions concerning Joyce's confrontation with Wagner and Wagnerism.[10]

Joyce was gifted with a fine tenor voice, an inheritance from his father—who also composed, for we know from the Holloway Diaries that in 1896 John Joyce "sang a tiresome, neverending topical rigmarole about 'Erin's Heroes,' written by himself."[11] (It would be interesting, in a stupefying way, to compare this with *Finnegans Wake*.) They shared the Dubliner's love of song, the range of young Joyce's repertoire stretching from the convivial and sentimental ballads of Ireland to Elizabethan songs and Italian opera. In 1904, not long after Bloomsday, Joyce shared the platform of the Antient Concert Rooms with John McCormack and J. C. Doyle, and sang so well that his future wife, who had newly met him, "formed the abiding impression, to the consternation of his friends in later years, that 'Jim should have stuck to his music instead of bothering with writing.' " The touching story is told of John Joyce's reconciliation to his son's elopement with Nora. In a village inn he sat down at a piano and "without comment began to sing. 'Did you recognize that,' he asked James, who replied, 'Yes, of course, it's the aria sung by Alfredo's father in *Traviata*.' John Joyce said nothing more, but his son knew that peace has been made." Also revealing is a legend that deserves to be true, of how Joyce and Franz Werfel carried on a conversation entirely in Verdian song. Joyce continued vocal lessons into his years in Trieste, and in 1909 he sang at a concert in the quintet from *Die Meistersinger*. Though he disparaged the opera as "pretentious stuff," the fact of his taking part in this complex musical venture is an important piece of evidence. Few indeed were the literary Wagnerites who could do more than follow the motifs in a handbook or tinkle them on the piano—or pianola.

The listener is distinct from the performer in Joyce. As a young man in Paris, despite his poverty, he found his way to the opera and heard one of the early performances of *Pelléas et Mélisande;* but what he thought of it and what else he heard we do not know. We learn that in Rome in 1907 he fell into a state of apathy, largely attributable to uncongenial work and excessive drinking. "A memorial procession in honor of his old favorite, Giordano Bruno, failed to stir him, and he had no patience, either, with a performance of Wagner's *Götterdämmerung*. He was resolved to find nothing to admire." Rome is perhaps not ideal for Wagner, or Wagner for a hangover, and so this incident may or may not indicate a first lapse of interest in and admiration for the Meister, who, as we shall be observing, was often mentioned, always with respect, in the early critical writings. By 1914 he was apparently in full reaction: "Joyce had no patience with the current adulation of Wagner, objecting that *'Wagner puzza di sesso'* (stinks of sex); Bellini, he said, was far better." This, however, is part of a conversation full of downright or paradoxical or teasing opinions and may express no more than momentary irritation or desire to shock.

In 1919, when Joyce was at work on the Sirens episode of *Ulysses,* he had a conversation about music with a Zurich friend, George Borach.

> 'I finished the Sirens chapter during the last few days,' Joyce is remembered as saying: 'A big job. I wrote this chapter with the technical resources of music. It is a fugue with all musical notation: *piano, forte, rallantando,* and so on. A quintet occurs in it, too, as in the *Meistersinger,* my favorite Wagnerian opera. . . . Since exploring the resources and artifices of music and employing them in this chapter, I haven't cared for music any more. I, the great friend of music, can no longer listen to it. I see through all the tricks and can't enjoy it any more.'

Just about the same time, another associate of Joyce's, Ottocaro Weiss, also had a conversation with him. Joyce had read some of the Sirens episode to Weiss shortly before they went off together to a performance *Die Walküre*. "In the first act, when Siegmund sings the famous love song, *'Winterstürme wichen dem Wonnemond,'* Joyce complained that the song's melodiousness was in bad taste and said to Weiss, 'Can you imagine this old German hero offering his girl a box of chocolates?' During the intermission Weiss lauded the music with the fervor of a young Wagnerian. Joyce listened gravely and then said, 'Don't you find the musical effects of my *Sirens* better than Wagner's?' 'No,' said Weiss. Joyce turned on his heel and did not show up for the rest of the opera, as if he could not bear being preferred."

How is one to interpret this—as anti-Wagnerian? Without the context of the Borach reminiscence, the Weiss account might be so misread. As it is, one knows that Joyce is fatigued with all music, and touchy with the touchiness of a despot visiting the territory of a rival; that he is nevertheless present at a Wagner performance, and that he thought of "Sirens" as rivalling music in general and Wagner in particular.

Wagner reappears in connection with Joyce's last great musical enthusiasm, for it was in *Tannhäuser* that he first heard John Sullivan sing. Sullivan has recently recalled Joyce's amusing remarks on the opera: " 'What sort of a fellow is this Tannhäuser who, when he is with Saint Elizabeth, longs for the bordello of Venusberg, and when he is at the bordello longs to be with Saint Elizabeth?' " (The answer that springs to mind is: Stephen Dedalus' sort of fellow.) If a remark of that kind sounds like "Opera News on the Air," this sounds like an answer to the "Metropolitan Opera Quiz": "I've been through the score of *Guillaume Tell,* and I discover that Sullivan sings 456 G's, 93 A-flats, 54 B-flats, 15 B's, 19 C's, and 2 C-sharps. Nobody else can do it." Nobody but Sullivan could sing the notes, nobody but Joyce (between operations on his eye) would count them.

A few conclusions may safely be drawn: that Joyce early and late was attracted to Italian opera, especially Verdi and

Rossini; that he listened to Wagner as opera rather than as music-drama and that as an admirer of bel canto he did not belong musically in the Wagnerian vocal milieu; that his technical knowledge of music, especially of song, was considerable. To this may be added the observation that Joyce's opinion of Wagner seems to have followed the Parisian curve: enthusiastic, favorable, respectful before the War; estranged, belittling, contemptuous after. Before (to begin our transition from the musical to the literary world), he belongs with Mallarmé and Moore, Dujardin and D'Annunzio; after, with such anti-Wagnerites as Gide and Cocteau, Stravinsky and Maritain. George Antheil represents the circle of young friends and admirers around Joyce in the 1920's and reveals the tone of its musical conversation: "Joyce's madness was opera, preferably Purcell, but if no Purcell was available, just opera. On one occasion he even managed to drag me to the Paris Opéra to see 'Siegfried,' on which occasion I became violently ill at my stomach—which is the way Wagner invariably affects me . . ."[12] Sylvia Beach more quietly records the nadir of Wagnerism when she observes of Paul Valéry that "strange to say, he was a Wagnerian and, unlike Joyce, owned up to it."[13]

Joyce was a literary man as well as a musician, and in order to surprise him in literary Wagnerism it will be necessary to turn back to his early critical writings, those unguarded and amateur pronouncements that betray him as his finished works of art never do.

Already at seventeen, in a review of some paintings, Joyce appeals to Wagner as one of the heroes of art; a year later, in 1900, he turns the Wildean epigram, "Even the least part of Wagner—his music—is beyond Bellini,"—a significant acknowledgement of Wagner as a force in European culture, significant in its bearings on the essay in which it appears ("Drama and Life"—even the title having a Wagnerian smack) and perhaps beyond it, for the young Joyce goes on to write: "However subdued the tone of passions may be, however ordered the action or commonplace the diction, if a play or a work of music or a picture presents the everlasting hopes, desires and hates of us, or deals with a symbolic presentment of our widely related nature, albeit a phase of that nature, then it is drama." What is this but the application of Wagner's idea of the "purely human" *(rein Menschliches)* to Ibsenite practice? And to confirm our detection of a Wagnerian context in his thinking he continues on the next page thus:

> Every race has made its own myths and it is in these that the early drama finds an outlet. The author of Parsifal has recognized this and hence his work is solid as a rock. When the mythus passes over the borderline and invades the temple of worship, the possibilities of its drama have lessened considerably. Even then it struggles back to its rightful place, much to the discomfort of the stodgy congregation.

The artistic possibilities of myth—with Wagner immediately adduced as exemplar—and the rivalry of the rightful claims of art with the usurping claims of religion: much of the later Joyce is here already; what is needed is the promise of a reconciliation of myth with naturalism and the quotidian, and that comes before the end of the essay, and again with reference to Wagner, and Wagner alone:

> Epic savagery is rendered impossible by vigilant policing, chivalry has been killed by the fashion oracles of the boulevards. There is no clank of mail, no halo about gallantry, no hat-sweeping, no roystering! The traditions of romance are upheld only in Bohemia. . . . But the deathless passions, the human verities, which so found expression then, are indeed deathless, in the heroic cycle, or in the scientific age. Lohengrin, the dream of which unfolds itself in a scene of seclusion, amid half-lights, is not an Antwerp legend but a world drama.[14]

Joyce is not again to be so explicitly a Wagnerian ideologue. The essay on J. C. Mangan (1902) moves toward a profession of Ibsenite faith, though only after asking "the strange question which the innocent Parsifal asked—'Who is good?'" and only in terms reminiscent as much of *Götterdämmerung* as of *When We Dead Awaken*: "But the ancient gods, who are visions of the divine names, die and come to life many times, and, though there is dusk about their feet and darkness in their indifferent eyes, the miracle of light is renewed eternally in the imaginative soul."[15]

This direct influence of Wagner's music and ideas is found in the work of Joyce's early twenties, when he is still making scornful references to literary Wagnerites like Mallarmé and Catulle Mendès. To such unmediated Wagnerism may perhaps be traced the poem of the Valkyrie, now lost, which Stanislaus recalls as a "longer and more ambitious effort" than the poems in *Chamber Music*. As late as *Exiles* (1913-14), when one of the characters, Robert, plays Wolfram's song from *Tannhäuser* on the piano, we might think this the only Wagnerian touch in an Ibsenite play if we did not have Joyce's own notes to prove how naturally Wagnerian parallels suggested themselves in the depths of his imagination. He writes, for instance: "If Robert really prepares the way for Richard's advance and hopes for it while he tries at the same time secretly to combat this advance by destroying at a blow Richard's confidence in himself the position is like that of Wotan who in willing the birth and growth of Siegfried longs for his own destruction. Every step advanced by humanity through Richard is a step backwards by the type which Robert stands for." This, it will be noticed, is not a casual reference but a searching allegory of his own play and Wagner's. And later, explaining his title, the exile from Dublin recalls the work of the earlier exile: "Exiles—also because at the end either Robert or Richard must go into exile. Perhaps the new Ireland cannot contain both. Robert will go. But her thoughts will they follow him into exile as those of her sister-in-love Isolde follow Tristan?"[16]

But the influence of that most literary of composers on this most musical of writers, as well as being direct, was also mediated by literary Wagnerism. It is reckless to say that everyone that Joyce had to do with in his formative years, this side of Flaubert and Ibsen, was a Wagnerite, but I will chance it.

A backward plunge into national mythology is a frequent phenomenon in the nineteenth century, a mark of the confluence of nationalism and the romantic movement, but it came so late and with such concerted force to Ireland that it is arguable that it was given some of its momentum by the success of Wagner's recreation of the Northern mythos, and that Yeats and his associates were groping toward the idea of an Irish literary Bayreuth, an art-theatre for the people. From this aspiration Joyce stood sympathetically alien in his early days. It was not Stephen Dedalus but the fresh and attractive, though essentially servile, Davin whose nurse "had taught him Irish and shaped his rude imagination by the broken lights of Irish myth." Heroic mythology, Wagner's included, but especially the sort transposed from the Irish in such works as Standish O'Grady's *Cuchulain,* are made the subject for mockery in the cyclops episode of *Ulysses;* and in *Finnegans Wake* all Joyce's predecessors are seen to paint from a "cultic twalette" in "the hour of the twattering of bards in the twitterlitter between Druidia and the Deepsleep Sea." The creator of HCE and ALP only hopped aboard the last time round, and it is an altogether wilder carrousel.[17]

A later and more sophisticated Irish revivalism the young Joyce also rejected. Like George Moore he could not confine himself within the idiom of "Kiltartan" as used by Synge and Lady Gregory and the Yeats of the *Celtic Twilight*. Like Wagner Joyce was to be a mythical poet, and again like him he was to avoid the direct road into the folkish through acceptance of a regional and primitive idiom.

We know that Joyce read everything by Yeats, and the

novels of George Moore at least as late as *Evelyn Innes*—the one about the Wagnerian singer. To these must be added the name of a third Celt, their friend Arthur Symons, whom Mary Colum describes as "a sort of god of the younger college set because of his book, *The Symbolist Movement in Literature,* which we devoured . . ." This book, it has been asserted, is so important to *Finnegans Wake* that few if any of the references there to Mallarmé need have come to Joyce except through it. Joyce met Symons in 1902, and this is how Stanislaus describes the encounter: "Symons told stories of the poets and artists he had known, of Verlaine and Dowson, of Lionel Johnson and Beardsley, and hearing that my brother was interested in music, he sat down at the piano and played the Good Friday music from Parsifal. 'When I play Wagner,' he murmured, closing the piano and standing up, 'I am in another world.' " Joyce was young enough to consider this somewhat ninetyish at the time; and his comment on the plot of George Moore's novel *The Lake* (1906)—"She writes long letters to Father Oliver Gogarty about Wagner and the Ring and Bayreuth (memories of my youth!)" —shows a similar drawing away from the ambience of earlier enthusiasm. Like Yeats in the often-denied anecdote, Symons and Moore seem to be too old for him to help.[18]

But the three gods of the Irish firmament are still potent to draw him toward Mallarmé and the Symbolists (most of them described by Moore in *Confessions of a Young Man* and criticized by Symons in *The Symbolist Movement*), D'Annunzio (championed by Symons), and Dujardin (an old friend of Moore's): all were Wagnerites.

For the Symbolists Wagner is much more than a topic of conversation, more even than the greatest current cultural phenomenon: he challenges literature's right to exist, and he supplies by analogy the means of accepting the challenge. Already in Baudelaire—himself Wagner's first great literary champion—the conception of the poem as alchemical *opus* and "globed compacted" microcosm is present, and the key concepts of transubstantiation and *correspondence* are used—as more than half a century later they are to be used in the *Portrait*.[19] An art is needed that will transmute the base metal of experience into hammered gold and gold enamelling; an artist is needed who can read signatures and riddle the correspondences of things below to things above. At this moment Wagner arrives to declare total art: in the smithy of his soul this magician (how often, how universally he has been acclaimed or denounced under that title!) achieves a synthesis of the arts.

The rivalry of poetry with music (or, rather, with the composite art of Wagner) is a recurring topic in symbolist criticism and in Symons' book. "All the art of Verlaine is in bringing verse to a bird's song, the art of Mallarmé in bringing verse to the song of the orchestra": a saying dark indeed except in the context we have suggested. Always he avoids the old and vulgar notion of mimicry or the mellifluous, always he has in mind Pater's conception of a striving toward the "condition of music." It is thus that he can bring together solid Wagner and rarefied Mallarmé.

> Carry the theories of Mallarmé to a practical conclusion, multiply his powers in direct ratio, and you have Wagner. It is his failure not to be Wagner. And, Wagner having existed, it was for him to be something more, to complete Wagner. Well, not being able to be that, it was a matter of sincere indifference to him whether he left one or two limited masterpieces of formal verse and prose, the more or the less. It was "the work" that he dreamed of, the new art, more than a new religion, whose precise form in the world he was never quite able to settle.

And here, in words that Symons translates from Mallarmé, is the conclusion toward which the whole symbolist movement moves:

> Whence, it being "music which rejoins verse, to form, since Wagner, Poetry," the final conclusion: "That we are now pre-

cisely at the moment of seeking, before that breaking up of the large rhythms of literature, and their scattering in articulate, almost instrumental, nervous waves, an art which shall complete the transpostion, into the Book, of the symphony or simply recapture our own: for, it is not in elementary sonorities of brass, strings, wood, unquestionably, but in the intellectual word at its utmost, that, fully and evidently, we should find, drawing to itself all the correspondences of the universe, the supreme Music."[20]

It seems likely that Joyce got from Mallarmé, through Symons, the idea of a total literary art, analogous to Wagner's *Gesamtkunst,* in which musical techniques, musical effects, the condition of music, have rejoined a poesis finally free from the brazen alembic of the discursive and rhetorical. About this time, and later, Joyce frequently shows a preoccupation, sometimes as in *Stephen Hero* solemn and ninetyish, later in *Ulysses* half serious, half playful, with the occult and with esotericism. He is in good Wagnerian company here, but the point that needs to be made is that the symbolist idea of the sacred Book, as found in Villiers de l'Isle-Adam and Mallarmé, is a weedkiller of lesser esotericisms: the only hidden doctrine in Joyce is his own book tied with seven seals, his only limbeck the smithy of his soul; and the great forerunner and rival in achieving such a work is Richard Wagner.[21]

Joyce accepted Mallarmé's goal but not Mallarmé's way. An art of omission was not for Joyce any more than it had been for Wagner. That Mallarmé was capable of being followed is proved by *The Waste Land,* "the longest poem in the language," a musical ordering of symbols with astral intervals between them. But Joyce must, Wagner-like despot that he was, include fact as well as form, and subdue the territory of naturalism as well as that of symbolism.[22]

To accomplish this he had need of other models besides Mallarmé. Joyce often refers to the novels of Gabriele D'Annunzio, with surprising respect. Wagner appears as a character in one of these, and in another there occurs a prolonged reverie on a Bayreuth performance of *Tristan;* but it is hard to see what in D'Annunzio he found of use except the word and concept of "Epiphany."[23] It is very different in the case of Edouard Dujardin. The *telos* of the hermetically sealed work of Mallarméan art, organized from within on the analogy of music, without rhetorical or discursive stiffening-material, is "the book that does not admit of any signature," the blank page. The blank page was never the destination of Joyce's art—rather the book of "doublends jined" is an endless scroll with the world printed on it. He must therefore find some way of organizing large masses of "verbivocovisual" data without reverting to "littérature." Dujardin showed him the way, and it was a Wagnerian solution to a Wagnerian problem—the presentation of a "monologue intérieure" on the model of Wagner's endless melody, organized by recurring ideas and phrases on the model of Wagner's leitmotifs.

Edouard Dujardin,[24] born in 1861, the year of the *Tannhäuser* fiasco in Paris which provoked in Baudelaire's noble defense the first great document of literary Wagnerism, himself dominated its period of greatest outward flourishing in the 1880's as editor of the literary organ of the symbolists, *La Revue Wagnérienne;* went on to give first application in the novel of Wagnerian principles of organization in *Les Lauriers sont coupées* (1888); revisited Bayreuth in 1896, and expressed the first French cultural (as distinct from political) misgivings about the Wagnerian despotism centered there; disappeared into a sort of limbo of atheism and theosophy until the publication of *Ulysses* and Joyce's public acknowledgment of indebtedness, whereupon, as at the words "Lazarus, come forth," he reentered the literary world with a book, *Le monologue intérieure, son apparition, ses origines, sa place dans l'oeuvre de James Joyce* (1931), in which he looks out upon Joyce and backward to Wagner. He died as recently as 1949, having outlived all the literary Wagnerites with whom he had been associated—the three young pilgrims to Triebschen, Catulle Mendès, Judith Gautier, and Villiers de l'Isle-Adam; Houston Stewart Chamberlain, co-founder of *La Revue Wagnérienne,* later to share in the depravity of German political Wagnerism; Mallarmé, whom he introduced to Wagner's music and ideas; George Moore, with whom he travelled to Bayreuth; and Joyce.

Doubt has been thrown on Joyce's seriousness in acknowledging Dujardin—and Dujardin only—as his predecessor in the use of the interior monologue. In particular, Stanislaus Joyce thought that his own diary notation of the thoughts of a person falling asleep might have been the germ; and Mary Colum recounts how Joyce in a "sardonic and prankish" mood when badgered by interviewers "fished up an old French novelist" and "informed a credulous reading public that he got the whole idea of the interior monologue from him. The more people he was able to bamboozle with this bit of information, the more details he added, the more it became a real creation equal to a section of Ulysses." Finally challenged by Mrs. Colum, he was at first angry and misogynistic, then whimsical and pleasant; and "I don't think he put forward the Dujardin legend again."[25] What is more likely is that he gave up mentioning it when he saw that it nettled her.

For the documentation of Joyce's indebtedness seems convincing enough. His knowledge of *Les Lauriers* dates from 1903, his first sojourn in Paris. In 1904 Dujardin and Joyce both contributed articles to the Irish magazine *Dana.* Furthermore, Joyce's acknowledgment was not a frivolous one, but was directed to Valery Larbaud, a distinguished man of letters, whom he evidently convinced. Indeed, I hazard the opinion that his development from the symbolists through Dujardin may well have been a factor in his achieving a serious literary reputation in France at a time when his success in the English-speaking world was largely one of scandal. He was recognizable there as a literary Wagnerite.

III

Joyce sang, read, and listened to Wagner during his formative years; Wagner and Wagnerism impinged upon his mind and imagination in a complex of varied ways. It remains to see the process by which this banquet of experiences was absorbed into the system of Joyce's art.

First Wagner himself, then the symbolists, then Dujardin: that was the progression of apparent and discernable influence. The tone-poet, the word-poets, and the novelist all conspire to direct the young Joyce to the use of the leitmotif. As early as his undergraduate days we learn that his professor of French "read with delight Joyce's paper on *Cloches,* in which the style tintinnabulated to suit the subject; and when Joyce invented the term *idée-mère* as a French equivalent for *leit-motif,* he exclaimed happily, 'For that I will give you my daughter.' "[26] It is interesting to note that Poe and Wagner stand in the same juxtaposition for the young Joyce as they had done, many years before, for Baudelaire and for Mallarmé.

Recurring images and phrases, suggestive and "musical," are to be found from the beginning in Joyce, and are perhaps a mark of any highly wrought literary style: certainly the most conspicuous examples in the *Portrait* are more reminiscent of Pater than of Wagner. It is in *Ulysses* that Joyce constructs, as Wagner had constructed in the *Ring,* a major, an all-inclusive work resting upon carefully placed leitmotifs as upon steel reinforcements. There are more than 150 motifs in the book, and of its 768 pages I have found fewer than fifty without the sounding of at least one.

If space permitted, it would be useful to consider, in full detail, one specific and typical *idée-mère,* such as the motif of

Paddy Dignam—small, red-faced, a drinker, forgivable, forgettable, dead. Such, we may say, are the "notes" that comprise the motif, its germ-plasm. This is not one of the elemental and thematic motifs, like the idea of paternity or the Hamlet parallel; neither it is a momentary recurring sound like "Heigh-ho" or "Poulaphouca": it has in the Hades episode its moment of strong statement, but its other appearances are scattered and for the most part muted. This motif we would find to be, like many others, protean: some of its constituent notes are stressed, some dropped, some varied or inverted, according to the changing contexts of the motif's recurrence. Just as in Wagner (contrary to received anti-Wagnerian opinion) motifs are never simply repeated but are changed by addition or subtraction, by harmony and orchestration, by tempo and key, by a shift of dramatic or musical context, or at the very least (if apparently identical with a previous statement) by the passage of time, by recognition and the consciousness of looking back; so also in Joyce. Joyce's leitmotif system is far more thoroughgoing and elaborate than that of Dujardin, or E. M. Forster, or Proust, or even Thomas Mann[27]—and is comparable in the whole range of art to Wagner alone.

The leitmotif system of *Ulysses* becomes apparent even at first reading, and students of the book may find later on that they cannot see the ship for the tackle. A more general musicality has likewise been claimed for *Ulysses,* ever since it was compared to a sonata with two themes—those of Stephen and Bloom—introduced, developed, combined, and recapitulated.[28] A moment's consideration must halt that analogy. A sonata in eighteen movements? A sonata moving on (in Penelope) to something quite new at the end? I doubt if the book as a whole can be compared with any existing musical structure. The two nearest, and not very near, analogies would be *The Ring of the Nibelungen* and Alban Berg's *Wozzeck*. The fourteen divisions of the Wagner epos have (as the sonata has not) the fullness and scope of *Ulysses,* and Berg's succession of scenes, each having a deliberately imposed musical form, resembles the deliberate imposition of specially conceived styles in Joyce's episodes.

The musicality of *Ulysses* may be brought to focus in the episode of the *Sirens,* the one in respect to which Joyce himself challenged comparison with the best that music could do, which (we recall) was what Wagner did in *die Walküre*. Add to the two conversations quoted earlier a letter to Miss Weaver in 1919. There Joyce asserted that "each successive episode, dealing with some province of artistic culture (rhetoric or music or dialectic), leaves behind it a burnt up field. Since I wrote the *Sirens* I find it impossible to listen to music of any kind."[29] This disinclination was, of course, temporary, but it does direct attention to that uniquely musical episode, which has always drawn high claims and sceptical rejoinders.

Stuart Gilbert's chart, inspired by Joyce, describes the technique as that of *fuga per canonem*.[30] Let us concede at once that the nature of literature as a medium precludes the employment of fugue or any form of counterpoint in a strict sense: several voices reading different words simultaneously in spoken madrigal would be mere chaos. The claim must therefore be to an effect analogous to fugue. One serious attempt has been made to substantiate this claim. "The subject, which, reduced to fundamentals, seems to involve flight (fuga) and pursuit, is stated in the 'bronze by gold' of the barmaids. 'Bloowho' or 'Greasebloom' is the second voice, stating the counter-subject. 'Jingle jaunty' is the third voice and 'Tap Tap' the fourth. 'Rrr,' modulating into 'Pprrpffrrppfff,' completes the fugue. 'Done,' says Mr. Bloom as if conductor . . . ."[31] Again, questions arise, the crucial one being, are we talking about instrument-voices or theme-subjects? Each instrument or voice in a fugue would have its share in stating and developing each of the musical ideas. If "Bloom" is a subject, then "Greasebloom" is that subject in the voice of the Siren-barmaids; but if "jingle jaunty" is a voice, what is "Jingle Bloo"? Of the five voices suggested by Professor Tindall, four are onomatopoeic and hence suitable to the analogy as musical elements; but in the company, the sound of the viceregal procession, "imperthnthn, thnthnthn" would seem to fit better than "bronze by gold," and the claims of "Horn Hawhorn," "Clapclop. Clipclap. Clappyclap," and even "Wait while you wait. Hee hee" demand some consideration. Again, this scheme leaves out all the actual singing in the episode: Simon Dedalus's and Ben Dollard's are not listed among the voices, and "When first I saw that form endearing" and "The Croppy Boy" are not among the themes. And how can it be that Mr. Bloom should be conducting a fugue in which he is himself one of the musical subjects—and conducting without realizing it himself or being recognized by the others? Mr. Bloom's word "done" when he breaks wind while a streetcar clatters by, after leaving the bar and its music behind, may be the author's wry comment on all human music-making (and also, in the context, on Emmet's epitaph), but it is hardly the remark of a conductor laying down his baton. Much more convincing is the observation in Professor Tindall's earlier book: "The difference between music and literature is that literature, composed of words, has subject matter. In music sound is form, but in literature meaning is form. Aping music, literature may acquire an alien structure, or, at best, improve in sound and rhythm, the elements it shares with music. In his formal experiment of the Sirens, Joyce did not achieve music, but symbolized music and made a pattern of sound and rhythm like nothing else in the world."[32] This, of course, is the old symbolist claim to the achievement of "the condition of music."

An acute problem in the interpretation of this episode concerns the page and a half of "overture" at the beginning. (Fugues, by the way, do not have overtures.) L. A. G. Strong says of it that "far from whetting our appetite, it induces a blank stupefaction,"[33] and Gilbert quotes a similar objection by E. R. Curtius:

> These two pages of seemingly meaningless text form in reality a carefully thought out composition, which can only be understood when the reader has perused the whole chapter, and studied it with the greatest attention. The literary technic here employed is an exact transposition of the *leitmotif*, the Wagnerian method. But there is this difference, that the musical *motif* is complete in itself and aesthetically satisfying; I can hear a Wagnerian *leitmotif* with enjoyment, even though I cannot place its allusion (Valhalla theme? Walsungen theme?). But the *word-motif*, unintelligible in itself, acquires a meaning only when I relate it to its context. Of 'Horrid! And gold flushed more,' I can make nothing. Joyce has deliberately ignored this essential difference between sounds and words, and, for this reason, his experiment is of questionable value.

Gilbert is able to answer a good deal of Curtius's argument: "The first notes of themes, for instance the intimations of the *Preislied,* are equally fragmentary; their meaning and beauty can only be apprehended when Walther sings the complete song. The clipped phrases give as much pleasure relatively to the completed phrase as does the *leitmotif.*"[34] It is true: Wagner in his preludes introduces motifs without anticipating the dramatic action, and in his music-dramas he frequently gives preliminary and fragmentary statement to themes. Moreover, *Die Meistersinger,* the most vocal and songlike and hence the most musically congenial to Joyce of Wagner's works, does proceed in the way he states—and it does, we recall again, possess a great vocal fugue that Joyce knew as a singer.

And yet this "overture" does not have a Wagnerian feel: it is too spare and scrappy and short-winded, and Wagner never studied under Nadia Boulanger. Professor Harry Levin is surely right when he says that "the whole passage is not a contrapuntal development of the opening phrases; the phrases are an impressionistic condensation of the passage."[35] Neither does the episode as a whole feel like a fugue. Mr. Kain is right too in calling it (and *a fortiori* its overture) the "cadenza"[36] of *Ulysses*—a display of every literary device that is, or can give the impression of being, musical. Much less intellectual than any fugue, the effect of the music experienced by Bloom in the Ormond bar and of the Sirens episode as experienced by the reader is (to dignify it) one of *détente,* (to belittle it) a certain flatulence. We must remember that in the *Portrait* music belonged with the passive not the active, with "swoon" and not with "encounter." The child Stephen hearing "Dingdong! The castle bell!" is moved almost to tears "for the words, so beautiful and sad, like music"; later, the music of Latin prayer is spoken of as "lulling his conscience"; and it is after repeating some dreamy lines of Yeats that "a soft liquid joy like the noise of many waters flowed over his memory." This last passage points through Sirens directly to *Finnegans Wake* in its lyric aspect. But the Sirens episode itself provides its own self-comment. "Words? Music?—" the idiom is unmistakeably Bloom's— "No: it's what's behind." And what is behind? Before the end, Bloom himself makes two answering comments, which we may relate if we like to naturalism and symbolism. "Music. Gets on your nerves," he says, and adds: "Cowley, he stuns himself with it; kind of drunkenness;" but immediately thereafter he says, "All a kind of attempt to talk."[37]

In spite of the claim to fugal form, and in spite of the fact that what is actually presented as heard in the episode is a blur of Irish ballads, operatic arias, and miscellaneous sounds, the musicality of Joyce in this the musical heart of the book is largely a Wagnerian musicality. It uses a thematic prelude with some limited analogies to Wagner's; frequent and recurring quasi-musical motifs are employed in what appears to be a freely flowing quasi-musical continuum; it uses all the devices of "word-compounds, word-distortion, and word-suggestion, which seem derived from musical practices like chord-building"—Wagner being the supreme harmonist and chord-builder; and finally it achieves the effect, surely and decisively Wagnerian, of an "orchestral universe," of "an ordered yet rolling and softening sound-sea."[38]

This suffused Wagnerism, together with the explicit Wagnerism of the use of *leitmotifs,* does not by any means exhaust the Wagnerian character of *Ulysses.* Joyce uses *leitmotifs;* he uses them as a major agent of coherence; he does more: he combines them into an order of symbols, a grandiosity and totality of organization, a despotism of art, that outstrips even his great exemplar. Joyce's art, like Wagner's, strives for the condition at once of music and of myth. If the literary symbol is the Wagnerian myth writ small (Verlaine's Parsifal, Laforgue's Lohengrin being cases in point), Joyce re-expands the literary symbol into myths to rival Wagner's. His mode is, of course, comic and ironic while Wagner's is heroic and tragic; and so Joyce can safely supersaturate both his great mythical poems with scrupulously mean and mundane detail, a practice that would be improper in Wagner. But Wagner it was, more than anyone else, who showed the way to achieve scale and universality by a mythical method, whereby the artwork of the future interprets and reveals the present by the firm use of, or the yielding allusion to, the time-worn, time-resistant structures of myth with all their plentitude of meaning and suggestion. Wagner goes back to a mythical *Urzeit,* Northern and mediaeval in its coloring; Joyce is rooted in 1904 but makes of it a mythical everytime. When Wagner first wished to express the modern experience of restless alienation, he conceived of the Flying Dutchman, and, in *A Communication to my Friends,* made this folklore figure an example of a type that included Ulysses and the wayfaring Chrstian.[39] When Joyce wished (among other things) to capture an analogous effect, he placed his Ulysses squarely in the "rubbish world" of the present and approached all mythical parallels first by way of comic and ironic contrast. His fully worked out structures are anti-mythical and mock-epic in their initial impression, and as Professor von Abele strongly argues, all the "identifications" of characters with Hamlet, Christ, Odysseus, Lucifer, Icarus, Telemachus, Elijah, Pantherus, Moses, and so on, are quasi-identifications that quite fail to set up coherent sets of relations among themselves and so are to be regarded either as dramatic projections of the characters' self-delusions or as a "rinsing in the water of comic irony," a dwindling of mythopoeic extravagances into commonplace actuality. Every interpreter must come to grips with von Abele's common sense, as he must accept the "thick and solid sensuous world with which the novel greets the mind."[40]

But the mythical in *Ulysses* (and in *Finnegans Wake*) can stand after this admission. *Ulysses* is mythical in being a "world"—full, complete, intelligible, imaginable, suffused with wonder and surrounded by mystery. Let us admit that the pseudo-heroics of the Cyclops episode blare out as an uproarious parody of the sort of heroic mythology often called "Wagnerian," of the Standish O'Gradyism that Joyce rejected from the first. The heart of the myth that he retained lies in the relationship of Bloom, Molly, and Stephen, a relationship first inviting, then resisting codification (the world, the flesh, and the devil), but reaching finally toward the sort of completeness that the persons of *The Ring,* taken all together, possess. Joyce, too, has been so careful to remove all appearances of sentimentalism from his work that one might miss the important fact that he shares with Wagner a cult of the redeeming woman. Certainly, the side of Wagner that led to the conception of Venus and Elizabeth or of the two Kundrys is absent from Joyce—except on the last page of the *Wake*. But there is a good deal of Lohengrin and Elsa in *Exiles;* Penelope "turns like the huge earthball slowly surely and evenly round and round spinning—"[41] like Erda, perhaps; the figure of Isolde between Marke and Tristan comes increasingly to obsess his imagination. And in life (though substituting humor for high melodrama) Nora Joyce played Senta to his Dutchman.

Before leaving *Ulysses,* we must observe that Joyce makes of Wagnerian echoes and references themselves a leitmotif.[42] One of the earliest occurs in Proteus: "He comes, pale vampire, through storm his eyes, his bat sails bloodying the sea, mouth to her mouth's kiss." This (combined with the song, "My Grief on the Sea") is the Flying Dutchman at his most phosphorescent in Stephen's imagination. The passage becomes more ironic at every reading when Bloom as Ulysses gathers the Dutchman and Sinbad and all voyagers to himself, "these flying Dutchmen or lying Dutchmen," as he calls them, and, as the day wears on and Bloom begins to overshadow them all, the apocalyptic nihilism seeps away and *The Flying Dutchman* recurs in his memory as simply a performance of an opera—or as a journalistic metaphor. A tramline from the cattlemarket to the river— "That's the music of the future. That's my programme. *Cui bono?* But our buccaneering Vanderdeckens in their phantom ship of finance . . ." The last Wagnerian reference in the book is the fagged observation that "Wagnerian music, though confessedly grand in its way, was a bit too heavy for Bloom and hard to follow at the first go-off."

The gigantic in Wagner has contributed to the "gigantism" of Cyclops. In its heroic catalogues Tristan and Isolde (in Wagnerian not Celtic spelling) are listed and Isolde's tower mentioned; there is a reference to the revolution of Rienzi and to a German savant with the comic name of Kriegfried Ueberallgemein. The Kisses in Circe that "fly about Bloom, twittering, warbling, cooing" recall Parsifal's Flower Maidens perhaps, and very remotely the Voices of all the Blessed may suggest *"ces voix d'enfants chantant dans la coupole."* All the rest of the

Wagner passages in *Ulysses*[43] relate to *The Ring* and bear upon the association of Stephen with Siegfried. And so we have arrived by *ricorso* back to our first topic of discussion.

Walking into eternity along Sandymount strand, Stephen carries with him one of the things whose signatures he is there to read: "my ash sword hangs at my side." The ash-spear of Wotan, the "augur's rod of ash," and the sword of Siegmund reforged by Siegfried, coalesce in Stephen's ashplant and carry into it the connotations of spiritual and physical might, connotations almost always at war with the immediate narrative context of impotency or of potentiality unused. At its first mention the ashplant is taken from a "leaningplace," a word chosen as more limp than the usual "stand." Mulligan thereupon recites the Ballad of Joking Jesus, and, mocking Stephen as both Icarus and Siegfried, "he tugged swiftly at Stephen's ashplant in farewell and, running forward to a brow of the cliff, fluttered his hands at his side like fins or wings of one about to rise in the air . . . ." Stephen walks away, "trailing" his ashplant by his side.

The ashplant continues to be thus subject to the tensions of irony. In the Proteus episode we see the hero "resting" it in a grike, with equal passivity he thinks, "my ashplant will float away," and then at the end he takes it by the hilt, "lunging with it softly, dallying still." In Nestor, the history of Pyrrhus at Asculum brings to Stephen's mind "a phrase, then of impatience, thud of Blake's wings of excess. I hear the ruin of all space, shattered glass and toppling masonry, and time's one livid final flame." Icarus hovers nearby, and so does the promised end, the Götterdämmerung; but Stephen does not at this point include himself in his vision as an agent, still less as a hero; rather he counts himself with the Nibelungs—"then from the starving cagework city a horde of jerkined dwarfs, my people." This same immobilism, the note of the anti-heroic, continues to sound. In Scylla and Charybdis, again in an Icarian context, his stick is repeatedly thought of as a sword, but the contrast of myth and actuality is acrid. In Wandering Rocks, *"Sacrifizio incruento,* Stephen said smiling, swaying his ashplant in slow swingswong from its midpoint, lightly"; and, later, again fidgeting with his weapon, "Stephen went down Bedford row, the handle of the ash clacking against his shoulderblade."

"Burke's! Outflings my lord Stephen, giving the cry . . . ." An exit to nighttown with a confusion of personal possessions, including "ashplants." "My lord Stephen" is no hero yet, but when nighttown is reached, the sword is at last to be drawn and used. At the beginning of the Circe episode, "Stephen, flourishing the ashplant in his left hand, chants with joy the *introit* for paschal time," whereupon "he flourishes his ashplant shivering the lamp image, shattering light over the world." This is not, however, to be the fulfillment of the apocalyptic vision: the gesture of heroism is not now carried through into action, and almost immediately Stephen "thrusts the ashplant" upon Lecherous Lynx, whose obscene mind sees in it only a "yellow stick." Stephen without his weapon hardly figures while Bloom's fantasies are projected at length; but when at last he re-enters, the context of Wagnerian parody is unmistakable, for he "chants to the air of the bloodoath in the *Dusk of the Gods* . . .

> Hangende Hunger,
> Frangende Frau,
> Macht uns alle kaput."

And he is recognized by Lynch as "the youth who could not shiver and shake," that is, as Siegfried. When it comes the turn of Stephen's mind to dissolve in the swirl of expressionism, he cries, "Quick! Quick! Where's my augur's rod?" Here the runes of Wotan's power (or Daedalus's) predominate over the blade of heroic strength and courage. With more animation than he has yet shown (hectic or galvanic though it is), he "throws" the ashplant on the table, then "snatches" it up, as he moves ever nearer to his statement of self-identity, "non Serviam," and his battle cry, "Nothung!" and his act of heroic defiance: "(He lifts his ashplant high with both hands and smashes the chandelier. Time's livid final flame leaps and, in the following darkness, ruin of all space, shattered glass and toppling masonry.)" The forging and wielding of the sword issue in the destruction of the world by fire ("Dublin's burning! Dublin's burning! On fire, on fire!")

What the reader of Circe, in his drunkenness, takes to be an explosion is actually an implosion like the bursting of a vacuum tube: the scene may seem a heroic climax at the time, but on balance it must be judged a comic anticlimax. Stephen "abandons" his ashplant, and Bloom, unlikely Bloom, "snatches" it up and "marks his stride" with it as fantasy is dispelled and matter of fact reasserts itself. "Here is your stick," he woodenly says, but Stephen does not take it up; at the end of the episode we see Bloom as he "tightens and loosens his grip on the ashplant," a meaningless action that reflects the sloughing off of *mana* from that property. Thereafter Joyce can say "I . . . curry nothung up my sleeve."

It will be noticed that the Wagnerian motif is precipitately abandoned when it seems about to collide with the stronger theme of paternity. There is not the slightest reminder, when Bloom and Stephen are drawn together, of the young Siegfried's using his sword Nothung to shatter the ash spear of his grandfather: instead, "Preparatory to anything else Mr. Bloom brushed off the greater bulk of the shavings and handed Stephen the hat and ashplant and bucked him up generally in orthodox Samaritan fashion, which he very badly needed." And when Bloom asks Stephen why he left his father's house, "To seek misfortune, was Stephen's answer," in the idiom not of frolicsome Siegfried but of gloomy Siegmund. The very incompatibility of the two figures (like the similarly incompatible association of Stephen with both Daedalus and Icarus, both Christ and

Satan) is skilfully employed to direct attention back to the surface of the narrative and to prevent metaphor from solidifying into allegory, or worse, false analogy, or worst of all, false doctrine. But, in spite of this safeguard, one wishes that Joyce had done his exegetes the good turn of quoting one last line from *Hamlet*—Horatio's comment, "Twere to consider too curiously, to consider so."

IV

Such deliberate drawing, bending, and abandonment of parallels, such a deliquescence, a dislimning, a discandying of allusions—the quality praised by French literary Wagnerites as the *"vague,"* the *"stylistique de suggestion"*[44]—if present in *Ulysses* is omnipresent in *Finnegans Wake*. What has been asserted about the musicality of Joyce's art, his use of the technique of the leitmotif, his adoption of a mythical method, applies the more strongly to this last work, which indeed can only be read and described on such assumptions. But any such description must either include almost everything or leave almost everything out, for what in the *Wake* is not leitmotif, what is not myth? This brief examen will be content to take a preliminary look at that little *jeu d'esprit* in Joyce's later manner, *From a Banned Writer to a Banned Singer,* to follow with a few specific remarks on the Tristan theme in the *Wake,* and to conclude with some general observations on its innermost affinity to Wagner and Wagnerism.

In his later years Joyce was not easily recognizable as a Wagnerite. A French painter of the Wagnerite generation who had known Whistler and Fantin-Latour, Moore and Dujardin—Jacques-Emile Blanche—met Joyce about 1930, at the time of his greatest enthusiasm for John Sullivan.

> His conversation consisted of ill-natured comments, but of admiration expressed for an English [sic] tenor. Him he fol-

lowed from place to place throughout Europe, from Brussels to Rome, and even farther when he sang in opera. Joyce was indifferent to music itself, for his passion was centred on vocal music, which, he considered, had an intrinsic value. He judged musical scores solely by the standard of opportunities afforded for the human voice to make itself heard against the most advantageous background. Wagner and Bayreuth have little to offer, no doubt, from such a specialized point of view, that of the enthusiast for virtuosos in the Italian manner.[45]

The Wagnerian touchstone or litmus paper yielded a negative result to Blanche. Let us see what Joyce actually does for Sullivan—and with Wagner. By that time, Joyce had already published many exercises and even finished sections in the *Wake* style; to help Sullivan, who was having difficulty in getting engagements, he wrote *From a Banned Writer to a Banned Singer* in the new style, assigning a paragraph to each of Sullivan's great roles: here is *Tannhäuser:*

> Saving is believing but can thus be? Is this our model vicar of Saint Wartburgh's, the reverend Mr. Townhouser, Mus. Bac., discovered flagrant in *montagne de passe?* She is obvious and is on her threelegged sofa in a half yard of casheselks, Madame de la Pierreuse. How duetonically she hands him his harp that once, bitting him, whom caught is willing: do blease to, fickar! She's as only roman as any *puttana maddona* but the trouble is that the reverend T is reformed. She, *simplicissima,* wants her little present from the reverend since she was wirk worklike never so nice with him. But he harps along about Salve Regina Terrace and Liza, mine Liza, and sweet Marie. Till she cries: bilk! And he calls: blak! O.u.t. spells out![46]

The first rule of the *Wake* style is, whatever the context may also be, to make it Irish. Thus the Wartburg becomes the Dublin Protestant church, Saint Werburgh's, and Tannhäuser plays upon "the harp that once." The second is to take it down and lay it low: Venus is thus a *puttana maddona,* and Elizabeth and the Virgin become Liza and sweet Marie. The third, arising out of the second (and perhaps out of the first) is, to make it funny, and this by two means—by bringing in at every turn the two supremely funny things, sex and religion, and by a ludicrous drunken mixture of application and non-application, in what is being presented, between what (punningly) may be called the *tenor* (here Tannhäuser) and the *vehicle* (the sleazy intrigue between the vicar and his Catholic mistress). This is not satire, it will be observed, but a more purely parasitic art, clinging to *Tannhäuser,* taking its shape, nourishing itself upon it, and yet having a separate, alien, ultimately hostile life. Just as Aubrey Beardsley (an implacably gay mocker of heroism) in *Under the Hill* consumed *Tannhäuser* so as to make its every cell pure Beardsley, so this goes forth, champs its food, and spits out whatever cannot be converted into Joyce. Joyce is well nourished here, for sex and religion are the essence (though not the sum) of Wagner's grand opera.

These same qualities are present from the beginning in the work-in-progress that became *Finnegans Wake*. Irish, low, and funny is the *Tristan and Isolde* passage that Joyce published as early as 1924, which Mr. Hodgart describes as a "rich and comic fantasia, in a style developed from that of the Gerty McDowell (Nausicaa) chapter of *Ulysses,*" and as a "parody of Wagnerian romantic love in terms of Irish middle-class vulgarity."[47] When eventually it found its place (after much expansion, dispersion, and combination with other material) in chapter four of book two, it remained much the same in tone, the difference being mainly in verbal complication. The early passage has some dozen verbal Wagner-references, all but one (*brineburnt,* perhaps suggesting the fire-circled Brünnhilde) names of the three principals in the story, given without distortion except for the portmanteau place-name "Lucalizod" and the nickname "Tris." The final reworking has three times as many, including now "the big kuss of Trustan with Usolde,"

"Isolmisola . . . Trisolanisans," "thirstuns," "Narsty . . . Idoless," "Tricks and Doelsy," and the puns and anagrams clustered round the *Liebestod* here: "Exeunc throw a darras Kram of Llawnroc, ye gink guy, kirked into yord. Enterest attawonder Wehpen, luftcat revol, fairescapading in his natsirt. Tuesy tumbles. And mild aunt Liza is as loose as her neese. Fulfest withim inbrace behent. As gent would deem oncontinent. So mulct per wenche is Elsker woed. Ne hath his thrysting. Fin . . . ."[48]

Pure parody demands of its original only that it lie still and allow itself to be parodied. What was hyperbolic in Joyce's boast about the successive chapters of *Ulysses*—that they leave their style-substances burnt out and exhausted—is literally true of the *Wake*. The *Odyssey* is permitted to survive *Ulysses,* so is Dublin, so is the Roman Catholic Church, so even is Wagnerian music-drama. Not so with the *Wake*. The Dublin that survives it is a ghost town (hush, caution, echoland); the Church receives its cue to peter out, for the newer rite, long ago foretold by Joachim Abbas, is here; the world has disappeared back into the word. As for Wagnerism, the *Wake* is not like music, it is music; it does not use leitmotifs occasionally or habitually, it is comprised of leitmotifs; Wagnerian references do not adorn, they nourish. The difficulty of critical discussion springs not alone from the complexity of the subject but also from its transmutation into something not amenable to description—hallucination, cauchemar, ectoplasm.

The preponderance of *Tristan* is understandable. The Irishness of the story, though a matter of indifference to Wagner, registered with George Moore and Arthur Symons:[49] the latter wrote a play on the theme with celtic twilight laid on like eyeshadow, and the former sent his Wagnerian singer Evelyn Innes and her Irish lover (modelled in successive versions on Yeats and AE) on a pilgrimage to Chapelizod, Isolde's home, later to be the locale of the *Wake*. Moreover, the Wagnerian original treats of love with religious seriousness, providing inexhaustible food for the white worm of Joyce's pruriency. Again, Wagner's biographer, Ernest Newman, observed of this music-drama that it begins where it ends and ends where it begins:[50] musically it is ready to begin again like *Finnegan*. And, not least important, the sad name Tristan (and the related Diarmait-Diremood)[51] gives opportunity for the jocose author to sign his work with a name opposite to his own and to recall the motto of Bruno the Nolan, *In tristia hilaris hilaritate tristis*.

But the *Tristan* references do not exhaust the Wagnerian bearings of the poem. "Now listen," says, surprisingly, Emerson, "to a poor Irishwoman recounting some experience of hers. Her speech flows like a river,—so unconsidered, so humorous, so pathetic, such justice done to all the parts! It is a true substantiation,—the fact converted into speech, all warm and coloured, as it fell out."[52] That is one way of comparing *Finnegans Wake* to a river, the first and most natural way: recall its opening word, "riverrun," the washers at the ford in its most memorable passage, the river flowing to the sea at the end. But there are further ways, and one is to liken "riverrun" to the E flat major chord of the Rhine, out of which Wagner created the world of *The Ring;* to see in the *Wake* as in *The Ring* the "artwork of the future," and all-embracing composite art of "endless melody" in the form of a four-part cycle. Crashes of thunder, single in *Das Rheingold,* multiple in the *Wake,* identify the time of the prologues as an *Urzeit*. Or, to impose a little further upon that analogy, Wagner, like Joyce, speculated endlessly about origins and the inner shape of history and expressed his intuitions in myths, not only mythical schemes spun out into treatises like Yeats's *A Vision,* but myths fully realized as works of art: *The Ring,* like the *Wake,* is "all puddled and mythified." If the *Wake* follows Vico's division of world history into four ages—theocratic, aristocratic, democratic, chaotic, here again *The Ring* resembles it as no other major work of art does: *Das Rheingold,* all of whose characters are more than human, is theocratic; *Die Walküre,* with its few heroic doomed persons, is aristocratic; *Siegfried* is democratic, with its "purely human" hero perhaps modelled on the anarchist, Bakunin; *Die Götterdämmerung* is the supreme poem of chaos.

What Wotan sees is the substance of Wagner's poem—Wotan the "Allvater," who "haveth childers everywhere." The mind, to be sure, rebels against too facile an identification of the god Wotan with the plebeian HCE. In a sense HCE is the Minotaur at the center of the labyrinth (*die Welt ist alles, was der Fall isst*); in a sense he is like Fafner the dragon—

> Ich lieg' und besitze:
> Lasst mich schlafen!

in a sense he is the shapeless and uncanny enemy of Peer Gynt, the Boyg (translatable, by the way, as "humpy").[53] But a reconsideration of *The Ring* will find the figure of Wotan only a little less protean. As Licht-Alberich he is the obverse to Schwarz-Alberich's reverse; he is a tyrant who loves liberty, a creator-god who longs for annihilation; he is caught agonizingly between being and having.

It is here that the ultimate resemblance of Joyce and Wagner lies—in their total, despotic art, an art that lends itself to, that demands, a cult. Stephen's resolve to "forge in the smithy of my soul the uncreated conscience of my race" is realized in the works—happy Joyce to have been excused the ignominy of remaining triste Stephen all his life. From "battling against the squalor of his life and against the riot of his mind," (words that apply to all mankind perhaps but especially to these two), he achieved the stasis of the artist who "like the God of the creation, remains within or behind or beyond or above his handiwork, invisible, refined out of existence, indifferent, paring his fingernails."[54] If Joyce had been God, as he very nearly thought he was, one wonders if he would have humbled himself to death,

James Joyce in the Smithy of His Soul

or sat watching in eternal cycle the television show of his own creation. Hardest crux ever, a *Halsrätzel*.

Noises, names, words, hollowsounding voices, waves talking among themselves, the common tide of other lives, the murmurous multitude in sleep—all these terms, these motifs, from the *Portrait* anticipate the *Wake*. But what is the final meaning of "forge" in the *Wake's* context of puns and belittlement?[55] An Irishman for forger is Penman: perhaps the signature of all things that Shem the Penman is here to write are forgeries. "What do you think Vulgariano did but study with stolen fruit how cutely to copy all their various styles of signature so as one day to utter an epical forged cheque on the public for his own private profit . . . ."[56] Joyce thinks of himself as a vulgar young Wagnerian in Italy (Vulgariano) at the point of transition in *Ulysses* from epic to parody, from forging to forgery.

If the forging is no more than forgery, it is rather a sick joke at the expense of the disciples, from whom (like Wagner) Joyce demanded in life and after death a big investment of money, time, and devotion. I allow myself this last modulation from art to life, for Joyce and Wagner are similar not only in the mythical scale and depth of their conceptions: they also "lived lives of allegory," in Keats's phrase. Their early struggles in a hinterland of European culture, their marriages (Nora was a happier, more durable Minna), their exile, the demands they made on the time and purse of their friends, their egotism and empire-building, the grandiosity of their artistic ambitions, the time it took them to complete their projects and the completeness of that fulfillment, and, not the least striking of resemblances, the international and polyglot intellectuals that were drawn to them to make a cult of personality as well as of art—all these bring the two into a single, very uncommon, category: the culture-hero as total artist, totally fulfilled.

Mr. E. M. Forster puts the matter pleasantly, and what he

says about *Ulysses* applies to the whole of Joyce: "It is in every sense a formidable work. Even the police are said not to comprehend it fully . . . . And the citizen who does survive the ordeal and gets to the end is naturally filled with admiration of his own achievement, and is apt to say that here is a great book, the book of the age. He really means that he himself is a great reader."[57] But had not Nietzsche already said the last word about Joyceans? "It is *not* with music that Wagner has won the youth over to himself, it is with the 'Idea': it is the mysteriousness of his art, its game of hide-and-seek among a hundred symbols, its polychromy of the ideal, which has led and allured these youths to Wagner . . . . In the midst of Wagner's multiplicity, fulness, and arbitrariness, they are justified, as it were, in their own eyes—they are 'saved'."[58] The last words of *Parsifal* flood through the mind, the words inscribed in stone on Wagner's grave, *Erlösung dem Erlöser*.

7

FINNEGANS WAKE IN PERSPECTIVE

Clive Hart

Finnegans Wake is very long; it took a long time to write; it was written by one of the greatest novelists of the century. One has to remind oneself of these facts in order to be able to contemplate, without cringing, the ceaseless flow of books and articles devoted to it. There is more than a little absurdity in the industry with which scholars pursue the problems of a work which, despite its recent publication in paperback form, is likely always to be a mystery to the great majority of readers.

The industry looks imposing, and much of it is of high quality, but it includes more than a little fakery. An independent study of *Finnegans Wake* is difficult to challenge, and therefore easy to offer as a doctoral dissertation or barrier-hopping publication. Few people will be prepared to gainsay it, and those few will in any case be members of the notoriously cranky Joyce clique. . . . No book, perhaps, has ever been more conducive to suppositious criticism. Its great length, coupled with its obscurity, has made it a unique critical problem. Very few ordinary students of literature have read it, in any real sense of the word. (I do not believe that I have met more than a dozen people, other than professional Joyceans, who have read it from beginning to end—paying some attention to the sense.) Indeed, it is not only ordinary readers who are unacquainted with *Finnegans Wake*: one finds that professional critics rarely read it. This latter fact has made still easier the publication of a mass of critical opinion which is uninformed, speculative, or absurd to a degree unthinkable in the case of books familiar to a wider audience. Even Joyceans, if they are not *Finnegans Wake* specialists, can be fooled by jejune judgments and crude assertions couched in modern scholarese. Thus, in attempting to examine what has been written about the book, and to assess the value of the various interpretative techniques that have been developed, one is confronted with a greater proportion of valueless material than in perhaps any other literary field.

I do not believe that, in the present state of Joyce studies, it is possible to offer anything approaching a definitive "reading" of *Finnegans Wake*. For that reason I shall give most of my attention to methods of approach. The article is divided into the following main parts: I The critical progress, in which I trace in summary form the development of *Finnegans Wake* studies over a period of some forty years. II Some assumptions about Joyce's working methods and his attitudes to the book. III Practical reading and the possibilities of explication. IV The consistency of the text and the limitations of exegesis.

I

THE CRITICAL PROGRESS

Studies of *Finnegans Wake* can, I think, be usefully divided into three major periods. The first runs from 1923, when "Work in Progress" was just beginning, to 1939, when the completed *Finnegans Wake* was published. The second takes us from 1939 to about 1955, just prior to the publication of Mrs. Glasheen's *Census* (first edition).[1] The third continues from 1956 to the present.

During the first period a number of pioneering articles were published. The most important of these were the proselytizing pieces in *transition,* Edmund Wilson's article in *Axel's Castle,*[2] and the collection of a dozen critical studies published under the well-known title *Our Exagmination Round his Factification for Incamination of Work in Progress.*[3]

In the second period there appeared, apart from a large number of articles, one book whose influence on *Finnegans Wake* studies has been very great: *A Skeleton Key to Finnegans Wake,* published in 1944.[4] A part of another book—the last section of Professor Levin's *James Joyce*[5]—is still among the best summary surveys of the subject. A third book, Professor W. Y. Tindall's *James Joyce: His Way of Interpreting the Modern World,*[6] containing lengthy discussions of specific aspects of *Finnegans Wake,* has been less influential.

In the third period we have seen the publication not only of Mrs. Glasheen's *Census,* but also of Mr. Atherton's important source-study, *The Books at the Wake,*[7] and, more recently, an increasing number of "hard-fact" works, such as Professor Hayman's *A First Draft Version of Finnegans Wake*[8] and Miss Christiani's *Scandinavian Elements of Finnegans Wake.*[9] The publication of a specialist periodical, *A Wake Newslitter,*[10] begun in March 1962, has provided a forum for *Finnegans Wake* studies with the emphasis, once again, on hard facts.

During these three periods, taken together, it is possible to discern a critical progression away from generalities and towards an increasingly detailed examination of the text. Commentators in the first period were, naturally enough, concerned to explain the aims and methods of the book to as wide an audience as was prepared to listen. Joyce organized much of this effort in a deliberate attempt to have *Finnegans Wake* accepted and understood. A great deal of what was written at that time was of the wildly theoretical and tendentious kind that one associates with many of the younger writers of the between-wars period. Joyce was proclaimed the breaker of barriers, the leader of a movement towards a richer linguistic experience:

> . . . He has decorated the world with our human feathers, he has tinted the spirit with delectable colours of flesh, of stone, of earth, of wood, perhaps, even, of bier. He has provoked us, given us back the immense temptation of the world, on which we have been cast as on cream custard.[11]

Joyce's efforts, and those of his experimentalist friends and colleagues, helped to bring experimental writing to the notice of a reasonably wide public, but a great deal of critical claptrap appeared in print, and ultimately Joyce suffered a disservice in being ranked with the vertigralists, the sonorists, the paramythologists, and all the other second-ratists of the day.

After the widespread acceptance of *Ulysses,* after the recognition of that book's achievement, and above all after Joyce's death, it became less necessary to insist quite so histrionically on the seriousness of the undertaking in *Finnegans Wake*. Those who were prepared to pay some attention to it were beyond the stage of needing to be told in general what "Mr. Joyce" was trying to do with his "big language." After the public-relations campaign came the first full-scale attempts to present the book itself—to explain what in fact Mr. Joyce had said in his big language. An excellent account, and one of which Joyce on the whole approved, was given by Edmund Wilson in his now famous and lengthy review, "The Dream of H. C. Earwicker."[12] Both Wilson and Levin, whose book appeared shortly afterwards, assume that *Finnegans Wake* is meaningful, that it is rationally constructed, and that it will progressively yield its secrets to patient and reasonably well-informed scrutiny. They enunciate the major themes and describe the book's basic pattern, but they show also how a grasp of detail is necessary if the pattern is to have any genuine human significance. If any-

Finnegans Wake in Perspective

thing, they make *Finnegans Wake* sound rather too easy, but their approach involves a method of understanding which has, since then, often been lost sight of and ought, I believe, to be further encouraged at the present time.

Not long after these initial surveys there appeared the book which has probably had the most lasting effect on students of *Finnegans Wake,* and is likely to continue to have for some time to come: the *Skeleton Key.* Messrs. Campbell and Robinson attempted to provide a lucid translation in fewer words than the original, and to help the translation along with interspersed commentary. It has been natural for students to turn to this summary when beginning work on the book, and it is therefore probably true to say that almost no one working on *Finnegans Wake* at the present time has escaped its influence—an influence which is in some respects regrettable. The translations themselves are often enough at fault (if one assumes the possibility of a rational approach to the book—see below). This, however, is only to be expected of such an early and comprehensive attempt at understanding. Such mistranslations are in any case not very troublesome to the reader after he has grown familiar with the texture of *Finnegans Wake* and has learned something about Joyce's apparent methods of composition. Gross misreadings are quickly forgotten. What is not so easily forgotten is the overall view of the book which the authors present. Their interest in mythology and theology has led them to give great emphasis to the mythological patterns, the cycles of human development, the scheme of birth, copulation, death, and rebirth which encloses the whole. They place great stress on Joyce's use of the Viconian cycle of ages, and lead readers to interpret *Finnegans Wake* as a macromyth, a time-capsule, an expression of man's role as a member of the race, an explosion from the level of the racial unconscious:

> Running riddle and fluid answer, *Finnegans Wake* is a mighty allegory of the fall and resurrection of mankind. It is a strange

book, a compound of fable, symphony and nightmare—a monstrous enigma beckoning imperiously from the shadowy pits of sleep.[13]

These things undoubtedly represent aspects of *Finnegans Wake,* but it is, I believe, easy to give them too much weight.[14] The trouble lies in the blurred sense of understanding which one has when one first tackles the book (and, of course, for some time thereafter). One stands confronted by a mystery; there is a feeling of rite, of incantation; one suspects that Joyce is attempting subliminal communication, that he is using language magically. (This may be partly true but, as I point out below, I think the emphasis should be placed elsewhere.) It is very inviting to believe that one should simply accept the mystery; and in this frame of mind it is just as easy to accept the proposition that everything in the book is about the great mythological concerns of the *Skeleton Key*—that, in fact, these are the themes of *Finnegans Wake.* The recognizable human individuals in it are reduced to mere representatives of generalities. One is led to think, for example, of HCE as Everyman—but not in the sense that Bloom is everyman; rather in an abstract and generalized sense which plays down specific characteristics and emphasizes the universalities and the godlike. Despite statements by Joyce himself, claiming that the real heroes of his novel were the river and the mountain, I believe this view to be almost wholly mistaken. It seems to me—reading *Finnegans Wake,* as far as this is possible, with an innocent mind—that although it is denser and more highly decorated than *Ulysses,* it is, like the earlier book, *about* ordinary individuals in the present, and that the myths and legends have a relationship to it analogous to that which holds between *Ulysses* and the *Odyssey.*

We urgently need a replacement for the *Skeleton Key.* Summaries of some length have appeared in recent years—notably the chapter-by-chapter treatment in Tindall's *Reader's Guide*[15]— but nothing of the scale of the *Skeleton Key* has again been attempted. Tindall's own summary presents a bare outline which is sane, amusing, common-sensical, and often illuminating, but of insufficient weight to oust the *Key* from its position in the mind of the average graduate student.

Tindall's other book, *James Joyce,* is an attempt at macro-hermeneutics. The meaning of *Finnegans Wake,* as far as detail is concerned, is hardly discussed at all. He deals rather with the major archetypal, mythological, and symbolical themes. The analysis is more sophisticated than that of the *Skeleton Key* but it appeared I believe, somewhat prematurely. When the individual bits and pieces that make up *Finnegans Wake* are better understood than they were in 1950, or than they are at the present time,[16] a really cogent analysis may become possible.

In the more recent period, attention has been focused much more closely on the details of the text. The first full-scale attempt to examine the content of the book in a genuinely analytical way was Mrs. Glasheen's *Census.* The characters and their many roles are listed in alphabetical order, and those facts which Mrs. Glasheen thinks relevant are briefly stated. In this way Joyce's elusive transformations are pinned down and cross-referenced, and the reader is enabled to pursue the intertwining themes with much less effort. That the *Census* contains inaccuracies and omissions is only to be expected, considering the immensity of the task.

In the first edition, at least, Mrs. Glasheen adopted a fairly neutral position with regard to the interpretative possibilities offered by the text. This was the first major sign of a development away from the pushing of a particular line and towards an empirical technique. The second edition, greatly enlarged, is still basically neutral and factual, but Mrs. Glasheen has introduced a special reading into her lists: the belief that *Finnegans Wake* may be mainly about Shakespeare. All that one can say about this belief is that it is no more and no less provable than any other theory about the particular references of Joyce's language. In the second edition Mrs. Glasheen has included a lengthy summary of *Finnegans Wake* which differs in many important respects from the *Skeleton Key* and Tindall. Much of the summary is tentative and (due to limitations of space) unsupported by textual evidence. It includes, however, several valuable new insights into the general structure of *Finnegans Wake*.

The tendency towards detailed scrutiny of the text continued with the publication of Mr. Atherton's book,[17] which is witty, erudite, and perceptive, although it may be said at times to rely on a number of assumptions about the mechanics of the text that have to be taken on trust. Among the most interesting things in *The Books at the Wake* is the enunciation of a set of "laws" and hypotheses about the book, many of which are demonstrated in action in Mr. Atherton's analyses. *Finnegans Wake* is treated like the physical universe: scrutiny of the whole will reveal general principles which may be applied to the elucidation of particular obscurities. Mr. Atherton's adduction of literary references culminates in a genuine reading of *Finnegans Wake,* a reading which is urbane, humanistic, and many-levelled.

Since *The Books at the Wake,* particularity has continued to be emphasized. Professors Hodgart and Worthington attempted to track down all the musical references in their *Song in the Works of James Joyce,*[18] the bulk of which is devoted to *Finnegans Wake;* Mr. Dalton's articles[19] show that he is unlikely to miss a broken serif, let alone a case of wrong font; in the first part of my *A Concordance to Finnegans Wake*[20] I attempted to carry out, once for all, a fundamental if mechanical task. But perhaps the most significant, if not altogether the most satisfactory, publication in recent years has been Professor Hayman's *First Draft Version,* which has made available to all students a great deal of information about the genesis of Joyce's text.[21]

The present emphasis on detail is, I think, to be strongly encouraged. Hitherto, however, the bases of analysis have been given far too little attention, with the result that some publications, like Miss Christiani's *Scandinavian Elements* (which attempts to translate and comment on all the Scandinavian words and allusions in the book), suffer from the lack of any coherent methodology. Mr. Dalton has some very pertinent ideas about the bases of analysis which, however, he is not yet ready to publish. Mr. Senn and I tried to stir up a little controversy over the matter in the pages of *A Wake Newslitter*[22] but few people were prepared to enter into argument. Mr. Halper has laid down some valuable principles in the course of his articles,[23] but his publications have not often appeared in prominent places and have, as a consequence, had comparatively little influence. It is with the bases of analysis that the rest of my article is concerned.

II

ASSUMPTIONS ABOUT JOYCE'S APPROACH
TO *Finnegans Wake*

The critical attention briefly outlined above has been based on a number of assumptions, consciously or unconsciously held, about what Joyce was doing in *Finnegans Wake*. As I discuss below, I do not believe that it is possible to arrive at any definite conclusions about the meaning of the book by examining only the text, and accordingly I shall devote a little space to what these controlling assumptions involve.

The making of assumptions, even though they may ultimately prove to be absurd is, of course, in itself a sound method of investigation. As with scrutiny of the physical world, it may be profitable to set up hypotheses about the nature and purpose of *Finnegans Wake* in order to make some analytical progress. Too often, however, such hypotheses have been maintained in the face of plain evidence as to their fallaciousness or futility. Too often critics of *Finnegans Wake* have used the book to pursue their own obsessions.[24] This is not, of course, a phenomenon peculiar only to Joyce studies. Critics of Shakespeare, among others, have been quite as aberrant in their pronouncements. The difference, in the case of Shakespeare studies, is that there the plain sense of the text keeps pulling the reader back to the common center, whereas we have no common center to which to relate *Finnegans Wake*.

What, then, might be assumed about the genesis and purpose of the book and about Joyce's attitude to it?

(1) Perhaps the earliest assumption—one that was made at least implicitly by Harriet Weaver when Joyce sent her his early sketches—was that Joyce was mad:[25] the book was the product of a mind totally alienated from the world of ordinary readers, from ordinary users of language. It might, like the literary products of certain schizophrenic patients, contain amusing, even interesting and enlightening passages, but as a whole it might be ignored as an unfortunate aberration of a once-great writer who had lost the power to make effective verbal contact with his audience.

This charge is easy to dismiss—too easy. There may be some truth in it. Joyce was indeed somewhat alienated from ordinary readers and ordinary users of language. He had very little idea of the inevitable responses of his audience but lived in a critical fantasy world, unable to comprehend why his book should not be widely read and accepted. (He showed himself at all times to be a very poor critic, both of his own work and of that of others. His literary training was scanty and his sense of artistic values odd. Joyce's powers were confined to only one or two creative contexts, outside which he was worse than mediocre.)

This is not, of course, the whole truth about Joyce's attitude to *Finnegans Wake*. He did at times accept the realities, and protected himself with such statements as that the book would be understood after the passage of three centuries. But his distress at the poor reception accorded to *Finnegans Wake* in 1939 was genuine. He had made his book harder than he realized; he had partially failed in his aim because he did not altogether know what he was doing. To what extent the authorial intentions and aberrations should influence our own reading of *Finnegans Wake* must be the subject of later discussion.

Not only did Joyce make *Finnegans Wake* difficult, however; he also made it according to some slightly alienated linguistic principles. Joyce, like some other partially alienated writers—Lawrence, for instance—would accept reason only when it suited him. He protected himself from criticism on the grounds of his use of Vico by saying that he would not pay much attention to such theories, but merely use them for all they were worth.[26] In respect of the use of language itself, however, Joyce was less rational. The truths of philology did not interest him. He used only those theories which suited his purpose, which cohered with his own irrationally conceived picture of how the world was constructed. He used theories which bolstered his all-consuming superstition.

The adoption of such theories is of course unexceptionable as far as the internal coherence of a work of art is concerned. There is clearly no reason why a book should be philologically accurate in order to be a fine work of art. But Joyce went further than this. He not only used language in internally coherent ways, but also relied on some of those theories to establish the external relevance of his book—in order, in fact, to communicate with his audience. Joyce used language in ways which would work fully for the reader only if certain irrational concepts about the function of words were true. His belief in the magical function of language is thoroughly well attested. He told Straumann[27] that the reader should "let the linguistic phenomenon affect one as such," by which he seems to have implied that communication of some sort will take place even when the meanings of words, in the normal sense of "meaning," are not consciously apprehended. There is some truth in Beckett's assertion[28] that Joyce used words as things, that he subscribed to ideas of a racial linguistic unconscious. If the reader is to follow the lead that he often finds in the biographies, he will allow the phenomenon of *Finnegans Wake* to work on him without rational intervention. He will expect unknown words to stir him, just as the sight of unknown objects of archetypal form may stir him. This attitude to the text has been adopted by a small number of critics, of whom perhaps the most serious in intent is Sven Fagerberg, who published in 1950 a lengthy article entitled "Finnegan och det öde landet"[29] ("Finnegan and the Waste Land"), in which *Finnegans Wake* is related to the unconscious needs and drives of modern man.

Joyce was, however, a schizophrenic type. The above was by no means his invariable attitude to the book. At times he was capable of claiming that certain readers (such as Wilson) had failed to "understand" certain passages. He would even, on occasion, provide a glossary (as he did when writing to Miss Weaver about the opening passage[30]), or allow others to provide glossaries (as in Stuart Gilbert's contribution to *Our Exagmination*[31]).

This all indicates, I think, some small degree of alienation which may influence the reader's approach to *Finnegans Wake*. It is not so much the mystical approach to language that seems out of touch, as the frequent schizophrenic vacillations between the total commitment to the unconscious responses and the rational semi-repudiations of that commitment—the claim that explication and hard work are necessary.

(2) An even simpler assumption, made by countless hostile critics during the publication of "Work in Progress," is that Joyce was a charlatan. He threw language together into any old outrageous shapes and laughed behind the reader's back. This assumption is even easier to dismiss than is the first, but once

again it includes, I believe, an element of truth which I shall discuss below. There is a certain amount of irresponsibility in Joyce's approach to *Finnegans Wake.*

(3) A further widespread assumption, which attributes some conscious purpose, but little order, to *Finnegans Wake,* is exemplified in the *TLS* review and developed in D. S. Savage's *The Withered Branch.*[32] Joyce is looked upon as the exponent of destruction, the prophet of the modern social crack-up. *Finnegans Wake* reflects the crack-up directly: Joyce wrote the book to express the dissolution of the universe, and hence the association of materials in the portmanteau-words is, by intention, self-contradictory, self-destructive, fortuitous, based on unreason. A grandiose agglomeration of disparate materials has been produced by free associative methods. Thus, although the reader may here and there glean some local sense by a similar process of associative reading, it is futile to try to derive any coherent statement from the book as a whole.

A close scrutiny of *Finnegans Wake* will reveal that it expresses not dissolution but rejuvenation. Many explicators, however, persist in a destructive reading method which is almost pure free association leading to any and every meaning—and hence to no meaning.

(4) As assumption contrary to number (2), and perhaps equally self-protective on the part of the critic, is that Joyce was a master-mind, incapable of error (as Stephen says of his ideal artist in "Scylla and Charybdis"[33]). Many adulators during the twenties and thirties acted on this idea, and a good deal of criticism still appears under its influence. The master-mind assumption usually leads to the belief that in *Finnegans Wake* Joyce wrote about the whole of human life and history, and that in doing so he created a work of art perfectly unified, brilliantly coherent, endlessly intricate in its internal relationships and in its external relevance to the world in which we live.

This sort of gushing "appreciation" would hardly warrant separate attention as an assumption bearing on the nature of the book if it were not for the fact that it has led, in practical criticism, to a special working hypothesis: this is the belief, held in some quarters, that Joyce (in reality, I believe, quite ill-read and limited in intellectual scope, at least by the best academic standards) knew more than any other reader can ever hope to know, and that in *Finnegans Wake* everything interrelates meaningfully with everything else. I have discussed, below, some of the results of the assumption of endless interrelationship, while elsewhere[34] I have tried to analyze the sentimentality which is inherent in such a critical approch.

The positive value of this sort of attitude lies in the fact that it assumes Joyce to have composed rationally, with conscious control over his materials. It is therefore a useful corrective to the attitude, touched on earlier, which would rank him with those who play on the reader's unconscious or semiconscious responses. While I believe that there is evidence to show that Joyce often flirted with the attractive idea of magical verbal communication, it seems to me that the emphasis should be placed squarely on the lucid, rational aspects of *Finnegans Wake*. The best representative of the opposite extreme is no doubt Gertrude Stein, whose relationship to Joyce might be likened to that between Jung and Freud: the one basically mystical, the other, in his best moments, rational; the one receptive, almost gullible, the other restrictive, empirical; both aspiring to cover the whole range of human experience.

It is possible, of course, to assume rationality, great architectural skill, and brilliantly conceived internal coherence without finding that *Finnegans Wake* has sufficient immediacy to move or delight. The feeling that it is a work of brilliant but futile Alexandrian complexity seems to belong to many critics who are otherwise favorably disposed towards Joyce. Professors Goldberg and Prescott are in this category, while the attitude is seen in extreme form in a long attack by Francis Russell.[35]

III

PRACTICAL READING

How do the above assumptions manifest themselves in practical criticism of *Finnegans Wake?* One can find meaning in *Finnegans Wake* very easily—far too easily. It can mean whatever one wants it to mean, depending on one's notions about its communicative techniques. Before we can arrive at any useful conclusions about either the total meaning or the meaning of individual passages we have therefore to decide on the nature and limitations of those techniques.

In trying to discover how to read *Finnegans Wake* we are necessarily concerned with the bases of any form of verbal communication. The assumptions underlying normal discourse are brought to the surface for re-examination. It may be that *Finnegans Wake* should finally be thought of as communicating in more or less the same way as do other literary works,[36] but that does not at first seem to be the case, and some careful thinking is needed before the reader can feel confident in making such an assertion.

THE SEMANTIC PROBLEM: I—WORDS

Two distinct stages are involved in what has become the most common method of explication of the book. The first of these concerns the reader's assumptions about the reference of the words in the text. To what system or systems of reference should the black marks on the page be referred?

We are used to literature which displays a multiplicity of meanings, but we are used also to a publicly apprehendable surface. "Mary Had a Little Lamb" may be a political allegory, but it is also, for the uninitiated, a simple, comprehensible narrative. *Finnegans Wake* often contains such a surface meaning, but equally often it does not. The following makes as much surface sense as does "Mary":

> A baser meaning has been read into these characters the literal sense of which decency can safely scarcely hint. It has been blurtingly bruited by certain wisecrackers . . . that he suffered from a vile disease. (33.14)

This second passage, on the other hand, is likely to mean nothing at all to many casual readers:

> Ichts nichts on nichts! Greates Schtschuptar! Me fol the rawlawdy in the schpirrt of a schkrepz. (343.20)

"Mary Had a Little Lamb" calls upon an agreed system of signs and symbols. By common consent we do not go beyond these signs and symbols as we read. (It is possible, nevertheless, to withdraw one's consent, as I try to show below.) For much of its length *Finnegans Wake* does not seem to use any agreed system, such as that of "Mary." If we look with an open mind at the possible alternatives, we find that at least four different working assumptions may be made.

(1) We may retain the agreement where the black marks on the page are, as in the first example above, identical with the conventional signs for English words and phrases. Approximations to such signs may be interpreted in the same way, as one interprets, for example, the everyday pun.

(2) We may assume that *Finnegans Wake* is an amalgam of typographical bits and pieces drawn from various agreed systems, each bit to be interpreted in terms of the system from which it appears to have been drawn. The contexts in question include, of course, not only languages in the general sense, but also such things as proper names and the specialist vocabulary of any intellectual discipline.

Finnegans Wake in Perspective

(3) We may expand number (2) and assume that any sign or symbol in *Finnegans Wake* may be interpreted according to *any* agreed linguistic or other system with one of whose signs or symbols it is identical, or to which it approximates. (E.g., the form "See" might be interpreted at all times as English "see" and/or German "See"—sea, lake—and so on.)

(4) It may be assumed that *Finnegans Wake* is based on no agreed system or systems, but that its words should be thought of as having an irrational, mysterious, incantatory, or magical effect on the psyche, in accordance with some of Joyce's apparent beliefs about the function of language. Receptivity, rather than analysis, would then be the basis of reading.

Justification for any or all of these assumptions may be sought either within the text or from external evidence. I shall discuss, below, the criteria of consistency. For the present, here is an example to clarify some of the consequences of the various assumptions. Consider the words "aqualavant to . . . kaksitoista" (285-16, 17). These might be taken to mean:

(1) "Equivalent to . . . cack (faeces) and oyster(s)." The idea of "sit" is somehow involved (?shit).

(2) "Equivalent to, and washing *(laver)* with water *(aqua)* . . . twelve (Finnish, *kaksitoista*)."

(3) All the above, plus such words and concepts as: qual(ity), *avant,* ant, accidia, toy, etc. etc.

(4) "Kaksitoista" as onomatopoeia, totem-word, etc.

Provided that it is possible to distinguish the languages or contexts from which word-parts are derived, the second of the above assumptions may at first seem to be the most rational, but one is faced with the question of why Joyce chooses to use foreign languages instead of plain English. "Aqualavant" is simple enough: it makes possible a multiple pun. But what is the point of using Finnish *"kaksitoista"* instead of English "twelve"? No pun is immediately suggested. The word is undistorted Finnish. Here it may seem rational to give a tentative acceptance to the first assumption as well as to the second: *kaksitoista* is used because Joyce wants the various overtones of meaning which arise when we relate the word-form to the English language. That is to say, we are asked to supply pun-materials which seem relevant when a foreign word is used in an English context. But if the English overtones are relevant, why not accept those from any other language or context of discourse? Why not, in fact, make the third assumption?

THE SEMANTIC PROBLEM: II—CONCEPTS

At this point the second stage of the enquiry must begin. The questions are these: What kinds of thing are being said if those various assumptions are correct? Can the assumptions be justified or invalidated by the nature and quality of the ideas which emerge? To what system or systems of ideas should the meanings of the words be referred?

It might seem at first that the problem can be solved with relative ease by examining the coherence or otherwise of such meanings as arise and relating them to what we know of the meaning of the text where its sense is plain. That a solution is not so readily available may be seen from the following two examples of explication:

(a) Book II, chapter I, line 1, words 1 and 2:

> Every evening at lighting up o'clock sharp and until further notice in Feenichts Playhouse. (219.01)

It is clear that the opening phrase means "Every evening at precisely lamp-lighting time, and until further notice, in the Phoenix Playhouse" (assumption 1). But Joyce has distorted some words to add further meanings and, by implication, has invited the reader to add distortions of his own to the words which appear in plain English. Thus it is apparent that the play is to be about man's whole existence, starting from the Garden of Eden—else why speak twice about Eve? (*"Every evening . . ."*) Since there are two Eves in the phrase, it is to be presumed that Adam's first wife, Lilith, is implied in one of them, together with the Second Eve, Mary, while the expression "Every eve-" relates the idea of Eve to all women, daughters of Eve. But there is a further implication in the opening words: Every Eve suggests *Everyman* (a play). Therefore we have here to deal with a female counterpart of Everyman, which suggests in its turn the idea of change-of-sex, or even of transvestism (to tie in with changes of role elsewhere, especially with the pantomime sex-changes on which Mr. Atherton has commented[37]). If we look at the first two words in combination, we see that they contain the word "rye" (-ry e-). This recalls the rye-field which plays an important part in the discussion about Shakespeare (a dramatist) in "Scylla and Charybdis." Anne Hathaway tumbled Shakespeare in a rye-field. The tumbling is, of course, a function of the Eternal Eve. The allusion to sexual activity strengthens the suggestion that the play which is performed in II.1 is to be about Eve as Temptress. We know also that it is to be a play about eternal truths, because of the presence of the word "-very," which may be interpreted in its primary sense of truthful. Joyce, however, is not anti-Eve. He clearly sees women as creatures of some value, and it is a representative of Eve who clears away the debris after the battles between the men. Thus we may read the second word as the present participle of the verb "to even": Eve as the soother, the ironer-out.

(b) The word "hatache" in the clause "has a block at Morgen's and a hatache all the afternunch." (127.30). The simple reader may see here the primary statement "has a block (?) in the morning and a headache all the afternoon." But let us consider "hatache." This contains the letters HCE in a common variant order: CHE. We all know that these letters stand for Humphrey Chimpden Earwicker, who is the subject of the clause in question. What, however, is the meaning of the residue of the word: "hata-"? *Hata,* among other things, is a Japanese word meaning "flag." What is the significance of that? The significance is, in fact, hidden in one of Joyce's usual pieces of devious presentation. *Hata* is a name used in Nagasaki for the famous Nagasaki fighting-kite. It is so used because the kite carries the colors of the Dutch flag—these having been adopted during the seventeenth century Dutch operations in Nagasaki. The point about this is, of course, that HCE is often seen as a Dutchman—a *Flying* Dutchman (just as the Nagasaki-Dutch were sailors, and just as the *hata*-kite flies). HCE has eastern connections, as we see particularly in Book IV. If we move a little further east we are in the Pacific, from which kites may originally have been imported into Japan. It is well known that the Polynesians thought of certain gods, such as Tane, in personified form as bird-kites. Thus, if Earwicker has a "hatache" it is only because he is a hata-CHE, or kite-god struggling with the elements, just as the Flying Dutchman had to struggle.

The above are not unfair pastiches of the sort of explication being carried out in many quarters at the present time. What is happening in those examples?

First, assumption number (3) from page 151 has been made, in order to define the *possible* limits of relevancy of the reference of individual words. Potentially, any meaning drawn from any linguistic system may be accepted. In practice, of course, the limits are more restricted, since only those meanings are accepted which provide a coherent set of conceptual interrelationships. The coherence is, however, potentially limitless. Joyce, the master-craftsman, made *Finnegans Wake* so brilliantly and so inclusively that it is about anything that ever happened anywhere. Thus any reading is true, provided it has some meaningful link with some other idea in the context. The network of relationships may lead in any direction, though some relationships will be more immediate than others and may have more appeal to the individual explicator.

Such exegetical procedures amount, therefore, to a series of recognitions linked by association. Individual units of potential meaning, established by relating the word-forms to parts of agreed systems of signs and symbols, are automatically accepted as "readings" if they can be shown to form part of a coherent pattern. Coherence is the criterion, the shibboleth. Typically, we are shown a series of associations which returns to itself:

$$a = b = c = d = e = a'$$

Term "d," say, may be relevant only because it is a link in the chain. In the case of "hatache" we begin with HCE and we end with him (the Flying-Dutchman-god—one of HCE's best known manifestations). In the middle we have the fighting-kite whose value, in such an exercise, lies only in its linking function. The kite is, nevertheless, an essential part of the coherent pattern.

My two examples differ in at least one important respect. The first never moves outside the field of reference established by the "plain sense" of those parts of *Finnegans Wake* which can be read as we normally read "Mary Had a Little Lamb," while the second gets as far away from that field as possible, but uses the chain of associations to return, at the end, to the context of the plain sense. The comparative restraint of the first explication does not, however, make it necessarily any more valid. How far afield may one go in weaving coherent patterns of meaning? Later I want to make a plea for weaving as *few* patterns as possible.

We need to remind ourselves that such explicative procedures are peculiar to *Finnegans Wake* studies only because we choose so to limit their application. If we want to withdraw our consent to the linguistic and referential conventions in other cases, we can apply the same methods wherever we wish. Let us consider, for example, the first line of "Mary":

Mary had a little lamb . . .

If we assume that the words in this passage contain, let us say, anagrams of words in foreign languages, we may find that "had," read backwards, gives Sanskrit "dah," which means "burn." The word is reversed. The reverse of burning is coldness. Mary is therefore to be thought of as frigid. (Thus far the outward excursion; now follows the return to the plain sense, only a little heightened.) That Mary is frigid explains her association with the little lamb and defines her identity more closely: a Little Lamb, the Lamb of God. Mary had—gave birth to—Christ. Both the BVM and Christ are, however, virginal, cold. This explication is, I suggest, entirely coherent. It is also very selective. Nothing indicates why we should read "had" in Sanskrit rather than in, say, one of the Papuan languages. As before, the potential meanings are selected on the basis of their coherence with the plain English sense.

Before we dismiss this as useless fantasy, we might examine a further example from *Finnegans Wake:* the clause "may the mouther of guard have mastic on him" (55.18). Reading the suggested English sense we find "may the Mother of God have ?mastic? on him." What is "mastic on him"? Mastication, perhaps, to cohere with "mouther." Thus: "may the Mother of God masticate him." We may, however, try as before to find further potential meanings in other languages, especially since the purely English reading seems to involve an odd phraseology at the end (though this might well be justified as a suggestion of Anglo-Irish speech). French gives one answer. "Mastic" means "putty." Therefore the clause reads "may the Mother of God have putty on him." A pun is now very evident: "May the Mother of God have pity on him."

Two issues arise here. First, what do we do with the putty? It seems to be only a link in the chain from mastication to pity. That is to say, it is, in itself, no more relevant than was the *hata*-kite. The second issue arises from the first: if putty and the kite are equally irrelevant, what makes the "mastic" explication more cogent than the "hatache" one? Nothing in the context of "mastic" tells one that the word is French. The answer seems to lie in Joyce's introduction into his text of further controls. We expect "pity" instead of "mastic" long before we reach the end of the clause. The question is how to get there, how to turn "mastic" into "pity."[38] In the case of "hatache" we do not expect from the context anything to do with the Flying Dutchman, or flying gods, however relevant these may be, in general terms, to HCE. The same applies to the general relevancy of Eve, etc., in "Every evening . . . ." Eve is relevant to *Finnegans Wake,* and she is especially relevant at that point, but nothing indicates that she is indeed included in the words "Every evening" except by orthographical accident. In other words, we have still to consider the question of internal consistency—of the extent to which the book is self-determining. It is possible to prove, as I think the above example demonstrates, that *Finnegans Wake,* or any part of it, is about anything at all. Such a conclusion is plainly useless. We can lead the text wherever we like. To what conclusions, however, can the text, in its turn, lead us?

IV

THE CONSISTENCY OF *Finnegans Wake*

The controlling consistency of the text is not always as apparent as it is in the "mastic" example. Internal consistency is, indeed, a dangerous criterion because of the vagueness of the word "internal." What is internally consistent? What is internal in a work of literature? Professor Tindall says: "A danger to be guarded against is free-wheeling interpretation. Your guesses about the meaning of any word or phrase must be justified by both immediate and general contexts. The text limits its interpretation. Not only ideas but tone and movement . . . can serve as limiting context."[39] This warning sounds sane enough at first, but it is difficult to put into practice when one comes to consider it in detail.

It is sometimes the case that the text itself indicates which of the potential meanings may be accepted, at least in so far as some readings make effective literary sense, while others produce only nonsense. This is not, however, always so. We must, I think, accept the fact that good sense—even profound sense— can be derived from any reading taken at random from among the limitless semantic possibilities, provided that it is handled with sufficient ingenuity. Since, therefore, the possibilities are endless, it may seem more useful to work at the other end of the scale: to accept only so much meaning as is necessary to make *some* sense of every semantic unit and, where there are several possibilities, to accept only so much as establishes the best sense.

It is a common experience of readers of *Finnegans Wake* to find that a tentative reading of a passage will later yield priority to another which is obviously the central intention once one has certain specific information at one's disposal. Such cases occur so frequently that one is tempted to generalize and suggest that if a reading seems doubtful it is probably wrong, or at least omits the most vital points. Mr. Halper's hypothesis that we should accept not *possible* meanings but only *mandatory* ones in order to understand the book[40] reveals a healthy conservatism. Unfortunately it is not possible to be so rigidly prescriptive about the limits of relevancy. The following example may illustrate the difficulty of finding an adequate criterion for the priority of readings:

> ... it came straight from the noble white fat, jo, openwide sat, jo, jo, her why hide that, jo jo jo, the winevat, of the most serene magyansty az archdiochesse, if she is a duck, she's a douches, and when she has a feherbour snot her fault, now is it? (171.23 ff).

Finnegans Wake in Perspective

What is "jo"? Is someone called Joe involved here? A case may be made out for the relevance of several Joes, including the Fat Boy from *Pickwick Papers*.[41] ("Jo" might mean something in a foreign language, but the reader is led to believe that an English reading of the word has at least some bearing on the passage.) Miss Christiani has pointed out that "jo" is a Scandinavian word for "yes," said in answer to a negative, like German "doch" and French "si." It is often repeated in speech, as in the present context. This, I suggest, is a "possible" reading, but it is by no means mandatory. The context does not suggest Scandinavian elements, and so we are not helped by the consistency of the text. Nor are we led, as with "mastic," to expect a meaning to which the form "jo" might be referred.

But let us reconsider the context. It contains at least two quasi-Hungarian words: "magyansty" and "feherbour" (the latter representing fever-inducing "fehérbor"—white wine.) Might "jo" therefore be Hungarian? Yes, "jó" is Hungarian for "good." Now it has come to be assumed by many Joyceans that in the light of such evidence "good" is in some sense a more "correct" and more valuable reading than "yes." We are not, however, led to *expect* the idea of "good" any more than we expect "yes." The assumption is an arbitrary one and requires examination.

There are some simple cases where it is obviously justified by results. One such is the following passage which has been explicated by Mr. Halper:[42]

> any vet or inhanger in ous sot's social can see the seen for seemself, a wee ftofty od room, the cheery spluttered on the one karrig, a darka disheen of voos from Dalbania, any gotsquantity of racky . . . (114.22 ff)

Recourse to an Albanian dictionary (following the hint in "Dalbania") elucidates most of the obscure words in this passage. No one, I think, will quarrel with the statement that the two most obviously useful senses of these words are those which are derived from our reading them as (1) English, and (2) Albanian. But when we start applying the technique to a passage like that on page 171 which I have been discussing, it becomes less obvious that one should apply the arbitrary rule "Read odd-looking forms in the language alluded to in the context." The principle is excellent when, as in the Albanian passage, we immediately see a whole pattern of meaning emerge. But in the case of "jo" it is by no means clear that "good" is intrinsically more meaningful, more valuable, more illuminating, than "yes." The fact that Scandinavian elements do not occur elsewhere in the passage seems to be no more than an arbitrary and remarkably artificial criterion. I believe that this rule of explication, like all others associated with exegesis of *Finnegans Wake,* should be applied only when and if it provides answers. Pragmatism is the basis of the world of the book just as it is the basis of Joyce's compositional techniques—indeed, of his whole practical philosophy of living. Too often one hears statements like this: "The word 'jo' is *not* 'yes'; it is Hungarian for 'good.' " Such statements seem to me to be as offensively prescriptive/proscriptive (and to show as little understanding of the function of literature) as those which tell us once and for all what the honey "means" in Yeats.

Furthermore, we need to come to terms with some of Joyce's expressed views concerning at least one point of explication—views that are far from limiting. In his letter to Miss Weaver dated 15 November 1926[43] he says, of the word "violer" (3.04): "viola in all moods and senses." It would seem that in this case at least, all of the *possible* meanings from among which Mr. Halper would choose only the essential, are relevant and "correct," in the opinion of the author. If this is the case with "violer," what is to be our attitude to the rest of the text? It seems that, if we are to give any weight at all to Joyce's opinion about his work, the only satisfactory solution to the problem is to accept, in theory, all the potential meanings with which we have been dealing, but if possible to arrange them in a hierarchy. Some are plainly more helpful than others, and in some cases one reading is by so much the most important that the others need hardly be considered. Let us retain "all moods and senses" as an aura of connotation, but in the present state of our understanding of *Finnegans Wake* we would do well to confine most of our attention to the kernel of meaning.

It is interesting that, in the passage quoted above, Professor Tindall should use the words "your *guesses*." One wonders how far *Finnegans Wake* may profitably be read by the guesser, how much research and specialist knowledge are necessary. I have dealt with this subject elsewhere,[44] but some of the issues need further attention. If internal consistency is to be a criterion, what are we to do when the consistency of the text is interrupted? *Finnegans Wake* has, like *Ulysses*,[45] a fractured surface. Intentionalism may be undesirable when we are discussing meaning, but when we are concerned with the accuracy of the text it is of some importance. We are wholly dependent on the author's arbitration as to what black marks are to be read on the page before us, yet in the case of *Finnegans Wake* there is often more than a little doubt as to what those marks should be and, more important, Joyce seems at times to have renounced his control over the marks.

It appears almost certain that Joyce intended some flaws to appear in the texture. The book itself deals with man's place in a fallen and broken universe. The cracked world can, unlike Humpty Dumpty's shell, be put back together again, but man experiences it only in its broken form—except, perhaps, for a few brief moments of blissful insight. The process whereby *Finnegans Wake* reached its final form was not unlike the process of the painting of Gulley Jimson's "Creation." It crumbled during the very moments of composition. While Joyce was elaborating successive drafts, his typists and printers were simultaneously corrupting and simplifying them.[46] Joyce seems to have taken very little account of many of these corruptions—

partly, no doubt, due to poor eyesight; partly, perhaps, due to a genuine artistic principle which led him to incorporate fortuitous materials, thus releasing the book to some extent from the artist's control;[47] partly, it may be, due to artistic irresponsibility or charlatanry. Joyce was not very energetic during the period of the book's composition. Although he took *Finnegans Wake* very seriously, he was by no means the devoted artist, the slave to his calling that some adulators have supposed him to have been. I make these points in order to emphasize the difficulty of knowing, in many places, what black marks should appear on the page. In the simplest sense of the term, some, at least, of *Finnegans Wake* may lack control; Joyce may have abandoned it to chance.

Quite apart from the critical questions which such a possibility raises, uncertainty as to the exact nature of the text often defeats any attempt to use consistency as the criterion of readings. As with some questions of modern physical theory, it is not that we could know but don't; it is rather that the information, the certainty, that we are seeking does not exist. Mr. Dalton has documented an interesting example of textual doubt in the word "barnaboy" (237.15).[48] This form is due to a corruption, and one which Joyce himself introduced. The original intention was apparently to write "baruaboy"—"barua" being Swahili for "letter." But Joyce misread his own handwriting. The error has completely obscured the original "barua." Is the Swahili for "letter" present in the text as it now stands? If we decide that it is not, what is the meaning of "barnaboy"? Should we read, for example, Swedish "barn" (= child)? If Joyce misread "barna" for "barua" he probably thought of the pun on "barn." It is certainly coherent with "boy."

There are numberless "errors" of this type, introduced either by Joyce himself, or by his printers and assistants. Nevertheless, Joyce approved the text after he had drawn up the "Corrections of Misprints"[49]—few of which touch on the sort of errors with which I am now concerned. When Joyce read and approved those corrupted passages, what did he think they meant?

Thus authorial irresponsibility, forgetfulness, lethargy, quirky laissez-faire, or a genuine desire to relinquish artistic control for an aesthetic purpose, has led to a situation in which the rational methods of explication desired by Mr. Halper and (so far as one can tell) by Mr. Dalton, can be used to the full only when the heavy machinery of scholarship is applied to the mss and proofs—and even then a deal of doubt remains. A reading of the text produced by such scholarship is, of course, thoroughly artificial. What is the ordinary serious reader to do? I think we may postulate, as Professor Adams did for *Ulysses,* that the fractured surface is a part of the art-work rather than a flaw in it. Joyce's artistic methods, which include irresponsibility and the *ça marche* shrug, may not be attractive to all readers, but we need, I think, to take *Finnegans Wake* on its own terms. Sometimes the consistency of the text will lead to precise answers, separating the essential very clearly from the peripheral. Sometimes, on the other hand, no such precision is attainable and we would do well to make what we can of the flux.

One of the commonplaces of *Finnegans Wake* commentary is a comparison of the book with a prose palimpsest, each layer of which is ultimately discernible, although some of the layers may be more readily apparent than others. It is also commonly objected that the multiplicity of layers of meaning which Joyce added to his text has in many instances rendered some of the earlier meanings of his words so obscure as to detract from the richness and impact of the book. Professor Litz makes such criticism in his commentary on "Anna Livia":

> "I warrant that's why she murrayed her mirror. She did? Mersey me!"
> Here Joyce has introduced the Mersey and the Murray, a river in South Australia: but in doing so he has almost com-

pletely obscured the original (and more important) meaning of "muddied." Similarly, on the first carbon he inserted Cher by converting "she must have turned" to "she must have charred"; changed "in which of her mouths" to "in whelk of her mouths," thus incorporating a "whelk" and the Elk river of Tennessee; and altered "nose" to "naze," the term for a headland or promontory. In each of these cases the original meaning was greatly obscured by the additional allusion.[50]

While I think that such criticism may often be justified, it is perhaps rather too cerebral and analytical as a general principle. Once again the idea of the fractured or distorted surface needs to be invoked. Like the universe, *Finnegans Wake* has weathered. As in descriptions of the universe, so with commentary on the book, we need to introduce a time-factor. Some things *were once* there but are so no longer. Only an outline or an occasional fragment is left to witness to features which have been superseded. (And, as I suggested above, sometimes Joyce carried out the weathering process himself, while at other times he allowed it to happen outside his control.) I use this analogy because many critics argue, as Professor Litz does, that "muddied," for example, is still present in "murrayed," "she must have turned" in "she must have charred," etc. I think, on the contrary, that they are no longer there, and that there is no need to criticize Joyce adversely for having let them wear away. The outlines and fragments of past forms may hint at the way the world of *Finnegans Wake* used to look, but the reader will be doing the book more justice if he immerses himself in what is there now (including the old fragments), instead of trying to reconstruct the past states. "Murrayed" means "murrayed" (turned it into the river Murray; made it a little masculine; married it; compared it to a murrain; left it with a faint suggestion of mud). "Charred," similarly, means "charred."

I would advocate, then, a rational method of explication which deals with the surface of *Finnegans Wake* as it now lies, but always with the proviso that reason shades off into doubt and ambiguity where the text is imprecise and badly weathered. I would advocate this method because it seems to me to produce the most stimulating results.

Finnegans Wake invites analysis, probing, and rational discussion. It also, however, invites receptiveness and immediacy of response. Joyce's polyglot shorthand is worse than useless if the whole is not greater than the sum of the parts. We may not be able to accept Joyce's half-enunciated theory that the book may communicate subliminally, independent of knowledge of the meaning of the words, but we ought to be very careful not to suppose that the task of understanding has been performed when all the details have been elucidated. *Finnegans Wake* is no coldly conceived deposit of human events. It is not a set of cultural annals in the David Jones sense. We should remember what Joyce himself said: "It's meant to make you laugh." Laughter is stimulated most immediately by the surface sense. In order to keep the balance right we must pay heed to the book's unique quality of tone and emphasis, created by its unparaphrasable juxtapositions. Perhaps that is what Joyce meant when he said "let the linguistic phenomenon affect one as such."

Notes

2. *CHAMBER MUSIC* AND ITS PLACE IN THE JOYCE CANON
Herbert Howarth

1. Richard Ellmann, *James Joyce* (N.Y.: Oxford University Press, 1959), p. 241.
2. *A Portrait of the Artist as a Young Man* in *The Portable James Joyce*, ed. Harry Levin (N.Y., Viking, 1947), p. 486.
3. Ellmann, *James Joyce,* p. 241.
4. This is the version in Joyce's notebook, as given by Ellman, p. 95, not the more elaborate version in *Ulysses* (N.Y.: Modern Library, O.S., p. 138).
5. *Letters of James Joyce,* ed. Stuart Gilbert (London: Faber, 1957), p. 231.
6. Ibid., pp. 318-19.
7. Ellmann, p. 119.
8. *The Critical Writings of James Joyce,* ed. Ellsworth Mason and Richard Ellmann (N.Y.: Viking, 1959), p. 89.
9. *A Portrait,* pp. 483-89, and *Ulysses,* pp. 48-49.
10. *Critical Writings,* p. 75.
11. Ellmann, p. 241.
12. Reprinted in Francis Hueffer, *Italian and other Studies* (London: Elliot Stock, 1883), pp. 106-25.
13. *Chamber Music,* ed. William York Tindall (N.Y.: Columbia University Press, 1954), pp. 25-26 and 214-15.
14. The reference is to "The Lover tells of the Rose in his Heart," the fourth poem of *The Wind among the Reeds.*
15. *Portrait,* pp. 493-94.
16. Ellmann, p. 108.
17. Ellmann, p. 143. In identifying the courtier and singer as the "ascendant" and in fact the sole performer in *Chamber Music* I

may appear to ignore the tintinnabulatory origin of the title, Joyce's frequent allusions to it, and Professor Tindall's sustained exegesis. In fact, the narrative of the origin confirms the view that the Two Joyces were thoroughly split at the *Chamber Music* stage. The grave Joyce occupies himself with the poems; the ribald Joyce with stories and jokes about them, which are sufficient sop, sufficient propitiation, to content him, and he leaves the other self to sing alone and undisturbed.

18. Ellmann, p. 358 (footnote*).

19. This and all the *Giacomo Joyce* quotations that follow are from Ellmann's *James Joyce,* pp. 353-59—exciting pages.

20. *Ulysses,* p. 254.

21. Ibid., p. 767.

22. Ellmann, p. 292.

23. P. 39.

24. *Letters,* p. 67.

25. Ibid., p. 259. It may be that the technique of sense-weaving is, *inter alia,* a tribute to Harriet Shaw Weaver.

3. THE JOYCE OF *DUBLINERS*
James S. Atherton

1. Gerald Gould, *New Statesman,* June 27, 1914; *Daily Courier,* Liverpool, July 3, 1914.

2. Ezra Pound, *The Egoist,* I, 14 (July 15, 1914), p. 267, reprinted in *Literary Essays of Ezra Pound,* ed. T. S. Eliot (London: Faber, 1954), pp. 399-402.

3. Richard Ellmann, *James Joyce* (N.Y.: Oxford University Press, 1959), pp. 227-31; 239-40; 320-21; 325-26; 334-35; 339-44.

4. Notably in Herbert Gorman, *James Joyce, a definitive biography* (London: John Lane, The Bodley Head, 1941), pp. 145-58; 169-74; 195; 204-9; 211-17; 219-21. Many of Joyce's letters to Richards and Maunsel & Co. are cited in full in this, which seems to be Joyce's account as given to Gorman. About four dozen of Grant Richard's letters to Joyce are in the Cornell Joyce Collection. See Robert E. Scholes, *Cornell Joyce Collection, a Catalogue* (N.Y.: Cornell University Press, 1961), items 1120-1168. Letters from George Roberts (a director of Maunsel & Co.) are items

1176-1188 in the same collection which also includes letters such as no. 1170 which is described as from "Alston Rivers, Ltd., London publisher, not interested in seeing *Dubliners* in 1908." (*Editor's note:* See Robert Scholes, "Grant Richards to James Joyce," *Studies in Bibliography,* XVI (1963).

 5. Letter in *Cornell Joyce Collection,* Scholes, no. 1297, from A. P. Watt.

 6. *Stephen Hero,* ed. Theodore Spencer (N.Y.: New Directions, 1944), p. 211.

 7. Ibid., p. 26.

 8. W. T. Noon, S. J., *Joyce and Aquinas* (New Haven: Yale University Press, 1957), pp. 60-85.

 9. Ellmann, *James Joyce,* p. 106.

 10. Ibid., p. 169.

 11. Marvin Magalaner, *Time of Apprenticeship, the Fiction of Young James Joyce* (N. Y. and London: Abelard-Schuman, 1959), pp. 174-80.

 12. *Letters of James Joyce,* ed. Stuart Gilbert (London: Faber, 1957), p. 55.

 13. Ellmann, *James Joyce,* p. 169.

 14. Stanislaus Joyce, *My Brother's Keeper* (London: Faber, 1958), p. 116.

 15. Herbert Gorman, *James Joyce,* p. 146.

 16. *My Brother's Keeper,* p. 74.

 17. Ibid., p. 104.

 18. Ibid., p. 52.

 19. Ellmann, *James Joyce,* p. 203.

 20. Ibid., p. 254.

 21. James Joyce, *Finnegans Wake* (London: Faber; N.Y.: Viking Press). All editions of this work have the same pagination and it is customary to give references to the page and the line on which a quotation starts. This is 585.34, i.e., 585 line 34.

 22. Ibid., 586.15.

 23. *My Brother's Keeper,* p. 181.

 24. Stanislaus Joyce, *The Dublin Diary of Stanislaus Joyce,* ed. G. H. Healey (London: Faber, 1962), p. 72.

 25. *My Brother's Keeper,* (Introduction), p. 19.

 26. Viking Press, N.Y., 1925.

27. *My Brother's Keeper,* p. 79.
28. Ellmann, *James Joyce,* Plate III, facing p. 80.
29. Ibid., pp. 18-19.
30. Ibid., p. 255.
31. Gerhard Friedrich, "Bret Harte as a Source for James Joyce's 'The Dead'," *Philological Quarterly,* XXXIII (1954, Oct.) pp. 442-44.
32. Ellmann, *James Joyce,* pp. 259-60.
33. See Marvin Magalaner and Richard M. Kain, *Joyce, the Man, the Work, the Reputation* (N.Y. University Press, 1956), pp. 64-7.
34. Ibid., 67-98.
35. Ellmann, *James Joyce,* p. 276.
36. *Letters,* p. 300.
37. Kristian Smidt, *James Joyce and the Cultic Use of Fiction* (Oslo University Press; and New York: Humanities Press, 1959), p. 43.
38. *Finnegans Wake,* 186.2.
39. Kristian Smidt, *loc. cit., Stephen Hero,* p. 80; Essay on Mangan in *Critical Writings of James Joyce,* ed. Ellsworth Mason and Richard Ellmann (London: Faber, 1959), p. 82.
40. Geoffrey Tillotson, *On the Poetry of Pope,* 2nd Edition (London: Oxford University Press, 1959), p. 115. Many of Professor Tillotson's comments on Pope's technique would apply equally well to Joyce's. "His descriptions are never simply descriptions" (p. 61); his "inspiration is always partly literary" (p. 88); he "paid unusual attention to the last paragraph" (p. 59).
41. Marvin Magalaner, *Time of Apprenticeship,* p. 136.
42. Magalaner and Kain, *Joyce,* p. 89.
43. Kathleen Coburn, ed., *The Notebooks of Samuel Taylor Coleridge* (London: Routledge and Kegan Paul, 1957), I, 1541 16.46.
44. Gorman, *James Joyce,* p. 147.
45. Hugh Kenner, *Dublin's Joyce* (London: Chatto & Windus, 1955), p. 49.
46. L. A. G. Strong, *The Sacred River, an Approach to James Joyce* (London: Methuen & Co., 1949), p. 19.
47. *Finnegans Wake,* 17.1.

4. *A PORTRAIT OF THE ARTIST AS A YOUNG MAN:* AFTER FIFTY YEARS
William T. Noon, S. J.

1. John J. Slocum and Herbert Cahoon, *A Bibliography of James Joyce,* 1882-1941 (New Haven: Yale University Press, 1953), nn. C 46, A 11, pp. 95, 18-19.
2. Peter Spielberg, "James Joyce's Errata for American Editions of *A Portrait of the Artist,*" first published in *Joyce's Portrait: Criticisms and Critiques,* ed. Thomas E. Connolly (New York: Appleton-Century-Crofts, 1962), pp. 318-328.
3. Ibid., p. 319.
4. Mary McCarthy, *The Groves of Academe* (New York: Harcourt, Brace, 1957), p. 210.
5. "First Publication of the Original Version of Joyce's 'Portrait,' " ed. with intro. Richard M. Kain and Robert E. Scholes, *The Yale Review,* XLIX (Spring, 1960), 353-369. The original handwritten Dublin holograph of this "Portrait" is among the Sylvia Beach papers acquired and now held by the Lockwood Memorial Library of the University of Buffalo. Cf. also the recent book edited by Scholes and Kain: *The Workshop of Daedalus* (Evanston: Northwestern, 1965), especially pp. 60-68.
6. *"Stephen Hero": A Part of the First Draft of "A Portrait of the Artist as a Young Man,"* ed. with intro. Theodore Spencer (New York: New Directions, 1944).
7. The appropriateness of Stephen's first name has often been pointed out: Saint Stephen, protomartyr (feast-day, December 26, the day after Christmas); Saint Stephen's Green, large public park in the heart of Dublin (facing Cardinal Newman's church); *Saint Stephen's,* the literary magazine of the old University College. I suggest that Stephen's last name *Dedalus* (or earlier, *Daedalus*) derives its special appropriateness for Joyce's imagination from Shelley's use of the name, more than it does directly from classic myth: for example, Shelley's "daedal Earth" (*Hymn of Pan*); "Daedal cups like fire" and "Daedal harmony," and so forth (*Prometheus Unbound*).
8. Quoted by Slocum and Cahoon, *A Joyce Bibliography,* E 3 (a), p. 136. Curiously, I do not find this letter in *Letters of James Joyce,* ed. Stuart Gilbert (New York: Viking, 1957).

9. Robert E. Scholes, "Joyce and the Epiphany," *Sewanee Review*, LXXII (Winter 1964), 65-77, here, in particular, 66, 76.

10. *Stephen Hero*, p. 213. Cf. *A Portrait*, pp. 212-213.

11. See, for example, *James Joyce, Epiphanies*, ed. Oscar Silverman (University of Buffalo: Lockwood Library, 1956), all the voices that Joyce here records, and in *Finnegans Wake* (New York: Viking, 1947), all the voices, the talk, the tunes, the names, and the many unexpected soundings orchestrated by Joyce into this much counterpointed score. As Joyce says, the scheme is like "your rumba round me garden" (*FW* 309).

12. A Jesuit colleague (Joseph A. Slattery) has suggested to me that a likely, amusing source for Joyce's Epiphanies, in the Greek sense, anyway, of the "nickname," is Ptolomaeus of Alexandria, and I sense from the so-called "Proteus" chapter of *Ulysses* that this is a sensible suggestion: "Remember your epiphanies on green oval leaves, deeply deep, copies to be sent if you died to all the great libraries of the world, including Alexandria?" (New York: Random House, new 1961), p. 40. Emerson and Thoreau were both much interested in the idea of epiphany as they found it set forth by Plotinus: see, for example, Joel Porte's recent book, passim, *Emerson and Thoreau: Transcendalists in Conflict* (Middletown, Conn.: Wesleyan Univ., 1966).

13. *The Secular Journals of Thomas Merton* (New York: Farrar, Straus, 1959), pp. 27-28.

14. See F. Pinamonti's *Hell Opened to Christians* (Dublin: Richardson and Sons, 1846); and James A. Thrane, "Joyce's Sermon on Hell: Its Source and Its Background," *Modern Philology*, LVII (Feb. 1960), 172-198; Elizabeth F. Boyd, "Joyce's Hell-Fire Sermons," in *Portraits of an Artist*, pp. 253-263 (originally, in full, in *Modern Language Notes*, LXXV, Nov. 1960, 561-571). According to *A Page of Irish History: Story of University College, Dublin, 1883-1909, Compiled by Fathers of the Society of Jesus* (Dublin: Talbot Press, 1930), Father James A. Cullen, S.J., spiritual father at Belvedere College during Joyce's stay there, was later, in Joyce's college days, stationed at the Jesuit Church of St. Francis Xavier, on Gardiner Street. There he was prefect of the parish sodality, and also had in charge the spiritual direction of the medical students at the Medical School on nearby Cecilia Street,—for all practical purposes, an extension of University College. *A Page of Irish History* includes the name of Father Cullen among those who were invited to come to

University College, during Holy Week or Passion Week, to conduct the Annual Retreat (Fathers Conmee and Bernard Vaughan were also so invited). Since the Sodality at University College did not hold its inaugural meeting until November 9, 1901, and since by that time Joyce had withdrawn from all pious sodalities, and no longer made retreats, the retreat sermons of *A Portrait,* in fact as in fiction, are most sensibly located, it seems, at Belvedere (where Joyce locates them), and where, in fact, he enjoyed the rare distinction of serving twice as the student prefect of the Sodality. In that position he was headboy, or captain, of the school. In composing the "hell-fire" sermons of *A Portrait,* Joyce's accommodations of Father Pinamonti's seventeenth-century tract *Hell Opened to Christians* may, of course, have been conditioned by what he remembered of Father Cullen's talks at Belvedere or heard about them at University College. See *A Portrait,* pp. 157-158; 421-422; 427-428.

15. I wish here to acknowledge my indebtedness to Mrs. Ruth von Phul for the assistance that she has given me so that I might isolate and with greater assurance express my own views about this sensed homosexual material of *A Portrait.* In an overall, now hard to isolate way, I am also much in debt here throughout to insights that came to me first from Mrs. Adaline Glasheen.

16. Kevin Sullivan, *Joyce among the Jesuits* (New York: Columbia University, 1958). See, too, for what it is worth my "James Joyce: Unfacts, Fiction, and Facts," *PMLA,* LXXXVI (June 1961), 254-276, and subsequent note, *PMLA,* LXXIX (June 1964), 355; and my earlier "Joyce and Catholicism," *The James Joyce Review,* I (Dec. 15, 1957), 3-17. I have commented briefly on some of the autobiographical materials of *A Portrait* in my entry on James Joyce in the *New Catholic Encyclopedia* (1966).

17. Jacques Mercanton, "The Hours of James Joyce," tr. Lloyd C. Parks, Part II, *Kenyon Review,* XXV (Winter 1963), 101, 111.

18. Mary Colum, *Life and the Dream* (New York: Doubleday, 1947), p. 94.

19. Ethel Waters (with Charles Samuels), *His Eye Is on the Sparrow* (New York: Doubleday, 1951), p. 220.

6. JAMES JOYCE IN THE SMITHY OF HIS SOUL
William Blissett

All quotations from Joyce are taken from the following editions: *The Portable James Joyce,* ed. Harry Levin (N.Y.: Viking Press,

1947), for *Dubliners* and *A Portrait of the Artist as a Young Man; Exiles,* ed. Padraic Colum (London: Cape, 1952); *Ulysses,* (N.Y.: Modern Library, 1942); *Letters,* ed. Stuart Gilbert (London: Faber, 1957); *Critical Writings,* ed. E. Mason and R. Ellmann (London: Faber, 1959); *Finnegans Wake* (London: Faber, 1950).

1. *Portrait,* 525.
2. *Portrait,* 311.
3. *Portrait,* 342, 354, 370, 381, 396, 407, 399.
4. *Portrait,* 414, 417, 418, 429, cf. motif of "serving" or "not serving"—370, 424, 487, 509.
5. *Portrait,* 430, 431; cf. "unfettered freedom," 517, and "soul free and fancy free," 520.
6. *Portrait,* 446-7, 488, 440; "swoons," 352, 407, 433; "ashplant," 493.
7. *Portrait,* 501, 507; *Ulysses,* 567.
8. Stanislaus Joyce, *My Brother's Keeper,* ed. Richard Ellmann (London: Faber, 1958) 112; W. B. Yeats, "Poetry and Patriotism," in *Poetry and Ireland* (Churchtown: Cuala Press, 1908) 4-5, 8-9, 10-11, 18.
9. George Moore, *"Hail and Farewell!" Vale* (London: Heinemann, 1914) 290-1.
10. The biographical material in this section is taken from Richard Ellmann, *James Joyce* (N.Y.: Oxford, 1959). The following passages must be especially acknowledged: Antient Concert Room, 174; Alfredo, 285-6; quintet, 278; *Pelleas,* 130; Wagner in Rome, 249; Wagner and Bellini, 393; Borach and Weiss, 473-4; Sullivan, 632, *Guillaume Tell,* 633. I have used passages from my review of Ellmann in *Queen's Quarterly,* lxvii (1960) 111-116.
11. Michael J. O'Neill, "The Joyces in the Holloway Diaries," in Marvin Magalaner, ed., *A James Joyce Miscellany Second Series* (Carbondale: University Southern Illinois Press, 1959) 104.
12. George Antheil, *Bad Boy of Music* (N.Y.: Doubleday, 1945) 153.
13. Sylvia Beach, *Shakespeare and Company,* (N.Y.: Harcourt Brace, 1959) 162.
14. *Critical Writings,* 40, 41, 43, 45, also 37.
15. *Critical Writings,* 75-6, 82-3.
16. *Critical Writings,* 104; Stanislaus Joyce, 101; *Exiles,* 168, 172.

17. For Irish Wagnerism, see Herbert Howarth, *The Irish Writers* (London: Rockliff, 1958); Ruth Zabriskie Temple, *The Critic's Alchemy* (N.Y.: Twayne, 1953); and my article, "George Moore and Literary Wagnerism," *Comparative Literature,* xiii (1961) 52-71. The quotations are from *Portrait,* 442; *Finnegans Wake,* 344, 37.

18. Mary Colum, *Life and the Dream* (London: Macmillan, 1947) 121; James S. Atherton, *The Books at the Wake* (London: Faber, 1959) 49; Stanislaus, 196-8; Ellmann, 116, 242-3.

19. *Portrait,* 488, 492.

20. Arthur Symons, *The Symbolist Movement in Literature* (N.Y.: Dutton, 1958) 5, 62, 73.

21. See Kurt Jäckel, *Richard Wagner in der Franzosischen Literatur* (Breslau, 1931-2) I, 129-183; A. G. Lehmann, *The Symbolist Aesthetic in France 1885-1895* (Oxford: Blackwell, 1950) 194-206; Kenneth Cornell, *The Symbolist Movement* (New Haven: Yale, 1951) 40 ff; John Senior, *The Way Down and Out* (Ithaca: Cornell, 1958). David Hayman's very full study of *Joyce et Mallarme* (Paris: Lettres Modernes, 1956) does not mention Wagner or Wagnerism.

22. Jäckel, II, chapter 5, shows that Wagner was admired no less by realists and naturalists than by symbolists, and exerted an appreciable literary influence on Zola and his school.

23. A chapter of *Il Fuoco* (1900) is called "The World's Bereavement": it describes the death in Venice of Richard Wagner in 1883; D'Annunzio's other Wagnerian novel is *Il Trionfo della Morte* (1894). Both these books were promptly translated, but Joyce very probably read them in Italian. The first section of *Il Fuoco* is called "The Epiphany of the Flame." Laforgue, in *Moralités Légendaires,* also gives a special sense to the word "epiphany." For evidence of Joyce's continuing high regard for D'Annunzio, see Ellmann, 60-1, 199, 275, 673n., 707.

24. There seems to be no full study of Dujardin's life and works. But see Leon Edel's introduction to *We'll to the Woods no More,* tr., Stuart Gilbert (N.Y.: New Directions, 1958) and *The Psychological Novel* (N.Y.: Lippincott, 1955); C. D. King, "Edouard Dujardin, Inner Monologue and The Stream of Consciousness," *French Studies,* vii (1953) 116-128; Aristide Marie, *La forêt symboliste,* (Paris: Firmin-Didot, 1936), chapter 3; Jacques-Emile Blanche, *Portraits of a Lifetime,* tr., Walter Clement (London:

Dent, 1937) 84-7; ed. and tr., John Eglinton, *Letters from George Moore to Ed. Dujardin*, 1886-1922, (N.Y.: Crosby Gaige, 1929); Dujardin's two books on Mallarmé and Symbolism (1919 and 1936), his study, *Le monologue interieure* (Paris: Albert Messein, 1931), and his article on Bayreuth in *Mercure de France* (August, 1896).

25. *My Brother's Keeper*, 16; *Life and the Dream*, 394-5; *The Psychological Novel*, 44; Ellmann, 534-5.

26. Ellmann, 61-2.

27. See my articles, "Thomas Mann The Last Wagnerite," *Germanic Review*, (Feb., 1960) 50-76; "Wagnerian Fiction in English," *Criticism*, v (1963) 239-260.

28. Ascribed to Ezra Pound by Richard M. Kain, *Fabulous Voyager* (Chicago: University of Chicago Press, 1947) 143. I have not discovered the passage in Pound.

29. *Letters*, 129.

30. Stuart Gilbert, *James Joyce's Ulysses* (London: Faber, 1930) 41.

31. William York Tindall, *A Reader's Guide to James Joyce* (N.Y.: Noonday Press, 1959) 185.

32. William York Tindall, *James Joyce* (N.Y.: Scribners, 1950) 124.

33. L. A. G. Strong, "James Joyce and Vocal Music," *Essays and Studies*, xxxi (1945) 101-2.

34. Gilbert, 239-40, translating and answering E. R. Curtius in *Neue Schweizer Rundschau* (Jan., 1929). The same question is discussed by A. Walton Litz, *The Art of James Joyce*, (Oxford: Oxford University Press, 1961) 68 ff.

35. Harry Levin, *James Joyce* (Norfolk, Connecticut: New Directions, 1941) 99.

36. Kain, 157.

37. *Portrait*, 265, 356, 493; *Ulysses*, 270, 283.

38. Terence White, "James Joyce and Music," *The Chesterian*, xvii (1936) 165.

39. W. A. Ellis, tr., *Richard Wagner Prose Works* (London: Kegan Paul, 1893) I, 334.

40. Rudolph von Abele, *"Ulysses:* The Myth of Myth," *PMLA*, lxix (1954) 358-364.

41. *Letters,* 170.

42. The Wagnerian passages that follow are to be found in *Ulysses,* 48, 470, 620, 469, 645, 292, 326, 303, 302, 466, 584.

43. *Ulysses,* 38, 49, 18, 20, 21, 45, 50, 51 (ashplant); 25, 46, 190, 208, 225, 238; (Nighttown) 415, 424, 425, 426, 547, 559, 560, 563, 567-8, 585, 593; "Nothung up my sleeve," *Finnegans Wake* 295; (Homecoming) 597, 604. Stephen bearing "Diaconal hat on ashplant" (682) has precious little Wagnerian relevance.

44. See note 21, especially Hayman, the second volume of whose study is subtitled "Stylistique de suggestion."

45. Jacques-Emile Blanche, *More Portraits of a Lifetime,* tr., Walter Clement (London: Dent, 1939) 281.

46. *Critical Writings,* 263-4.

47. M. J. C. Hodgart, "The Earliest Sections of *Finnegans Wake,*" *James Joyce Review,* i (1957) 4.

48. *Finnegans Wake,* 383-399, especially 388.

49. The second version of Moore's *Evelyn Innes* (1901) has an interpolated chapter in which the Wagnerian singer and her lover visit Chapelizod. Symons' *Tristan and Iseult: A Play in Four Acts* (1917) has a dedication to Eleanora Duse and an epigraph from D'Annunzio's *Tristano e Isotta.*

50. Ernest Newman, *The Wagner Operas,* (N.Y.: Knopf, 1949) 202.

51. Joseph Campbell and Henry Morton Robinson, *A Skeleton Key to Finnegans Wake,* (N.Y.: Compass Books, 1961) 106 n.

52. "Eloquence," in *Solitude and Society* (Boston: Houghton Mifflin, 1904) 68.

53. Brian W. Downs, *A Study of Six Plays of Ibsen* (Cambridge: University Press, 1950) 83.

54. *Portrait,* 340, 481-2.

55. W. Y. Tindall, *Reader's Guide,* 67; also Robert S. Ryf, *A New Approach to Joyce,* (University of California Press, 1962) 165-6. I believe that the word in the *Portrait* can have no sense of "forgery."

56. *Finnegans Wake,* 181; also 305, "Forge away, Sunny Sim!"

57. *New York Times,* June 19, 1949.

58. Friedrich Nietzsche, *The Case of Wagner,* tr., Thomas Common (London: H. Henry, 1896) 38.

7. FINNEGANS WAKE IN PERSPECTIVE
Clive Hart

1. Adaline Glasheen, *A Census of Finnegans Wake: an Index of the Characters and Their Roles* (Evanston: Northwestern University Press, 1956). Second edn., 1963.

2. Edmund Wilson, *Axel's Castle: a Study in the Imaginative Literature of 1870-1930* (New York: Charles Scribner's Sons, 1931).

3. Samuel Beckett et al., *Our Exagmination Round his Factification for Incamination of Work in Progress* (Paris: Shakespeare and Company, 1929).

4. Joseph Campbell and Henry Morton Robinson, *A Skeleton Key to Finnegans Wake* (New York: Harcourt, 1944).

5. Harry Levin, *James Joyce: a Critical Introduction* (Norfolk: New Directions, 1941).

6. William York Tindall, *James Joyce: His Way of Interpreting the Modern World* (New York: Charles Scribner's Sons, 1950).

7. James S. Atherton, *The Books at the Wake* (London: Faber & Faber, 1959).

8. David Hayman, *A First Draft Version of Finnegans Wake* (Austin: University of Texas Press, 1963).

9. Dounia B. Christiani, *Scandinavian Elements of Finnegans Wake* (Evanston: Northwestern University Press, 1965).

10. *A Wake Newslitter*, Clive Hart and Fritz Senn, eds.

11. Armand M. Petitjean, "Joyce and Mythology: Mythology and Joyce," *transition 23* (1934-1935), p. 142.

12. Edmund Wilson, "The Dream of H. C. Earwicker," repr. in *The Wound and the Bow* (Boston: Houghton Mifflin, 1941), pp. 243-71.

13. *A Skeleton Key*, p. 13.

14. As I myself did in my *Structure and Motif in Finnegans Wake* (London: Faber & Faber, 1962).

15. William York Tindall, *A Reader's Guide to James Joyce* (New York: Noonday Press, 1959).

16. A further attempt at a general conspectus, emphasizing this time Joyce's attitudes to authority, is provided in Helmut Bonheim, *Joyce's Benefictions* (Berkeley and Los Angeles: University of California Press, 1964).

17. Mr. Atherton has continued his own studies in this vein in "A Few More Books at the Wake," *James Joyce Quarterly,* II, 3 (Spring, 1965), pp. 142-49.

18. Matthew J. C. Hodgart and Mabel P. Worthington, *Song in the Works of James Joyce* (New York: Columbia University Press, 1959).

19. See the pages of *A Wake Newslitter* and *James Joyce Quarterly.*

20. Clive Hart, *A Concordance to Finnegans Wake* (Minneapolis: Minnesota University Press, 1963).

21. A more comprehensive account of the mss. of the "Anna Livia" chapter is given in Fred H. Higginson, *Anna Livia Plurabelle: the Making of a Chapter* (Minneapolis: Minnesota University Press, 1960). Other important ms. information is available in Thomas E. Connolly, *Scribbledehobble: the Ur-Workbook for Finnegans Wake* (Evanston: Northwestern University Press, 1961).

22. Clive Hart, "The Elephant in the Belly: Exegesis of *Finnegans Wake,*" *A Wake Newslitter,* no. 13 (May, 1963), pp. 1-8; Fritz Senn, "A Test-Case of Overreading," *A Wake Newslitter,* n.s., I, 2 (April, 1964), pp. 1-8. See also Stephen Barber, "Nichthemerical Litter," *A Wake Newslitter,* n.s., II, 3 (June, 1965), pp. 15-17.

23. E.g., Nathan Halper, "Notes on Late Historical Events," *A Wake Newslitter,* n.s., II, 5 (Oct., 1965), pp. 15-16.

24. The most outstanding example in recent years is no doubt the following violently anti-British book: Frances Motz Boldereff, *Reading Finnegans Wake* (Woodward, Pa.: Classic Nonfiction Library, 1959).

25. See, for example, Richard Ellmann, *James Joyce* (New York: Oxford University Press, 1959), p. 603.

26. Stuart Gilbert, ed., *Letters of James Joyce* (London: Faber & Faber, 1957), p. 241.

27. Heinrich Straumann, "Last Meeting with Joyce," in *A James Joyce Yearbook,* ed. M. Jolas (Paris: Transition Press, 1949), p. 114.

28. Samuel Beckett, "Dante . . . Bruno. Vico . . . Joyce," in *Our Exagmination,* pp. 3-22.

29. Sven Fagerberg, "Finnegan och det öde landet," *Poesi,* III, 1 (1950), pp. 11-40.

30. *Letters,* pp. 247-48.
31. Stuart Gilbert, "Prolegomena to *Work in Progress,*" in *Our Exagmination,* pp. 49-75.
32. D. S. Savage, *The Withered Branch: Six Studies in the Modern Novel* (New York: Pellegrini and Cudahy, 1952).
33. *Ulysses* (New York: Random House, 1934), p. 188.
34. Clive Hart, "James Joyce's Sentimentality." To appear shortly.
35. S. L. Goldberg, *Joyce* (Edinburgh and London: Oliver and Boyd, 1962); Joseph Prescott, *Exploring James Joyce* (Carbondale: Southern Illinois University Press, 1964); Francis Russell, "Joyce and Alexandria," in *Three Studies in Twentieth Century Obscurity* (Aldington: The Hand and Flower Press, 1954), pp. 7-44.

Due to limitations of space I have had to omit from this part of my article discussions of a number of books which are of the utmost value to students of *Finnegans Wake.* These include Father William T. Noon's very scholarly account of Joyce's theology: *Joyce and Aquinas* (New Haven: Yale University Press, 1957), and the chapters on *Finnegans Wake* in Hugh Kenner, *Dublin's Joyce* (London: Chatto and Windus, 1955), which are among the most brilliant on the subject. Mrs. Ruth von Phul is currently engaged in a highly interesting biographical study of all of Joyce's works.

36. With some reservations this is now my own view; see below.
37. J. S. Atherton, *"Finnegans Wake:* the gist of the pantomime," *Accent,* XV, 1 (Winter, 1955), pp. 14-26.
38. We might equally, of course, expect "mercy"; it may be possible to derive this sense from another language, using the same technique, in which case I would hold that both "mercy" and "pity" are correct.
39. Tindall, *Reader's Guide,* p. 265.
40. Nathan Halper, "Notes on Late Historical Events," *A Wake Newslitter,* n.s., II, 5 (Oct., 1965), p. 16.
41. See *Second Census,* p. 132.
42. Nathan Halper, "A Passage in Albanian," *A Wake Newslitter,* no. 14 (June, 1963), pp. 5-6.
43. *Letters,* p. 247.

44. Clive Hart, "The Elephant in the Belly: Exegesis of *Finnegans Wake*," revised version, to appear shortly in *A Wake Digest*, ed. Clive Hart and Fritz Senn.

45. See Robert M. Adams, *Surface and Symbol: The Consistency of James Joyce's Ulysses* (New York: Oxford University Press, 1962).

46. See, for example, Fred H. Higginson, "Notes on the Text of *Finnegans Wake*," *JEGP*, LV, 3 (July, 1956), pp. 451-56.

47. Cf. the story about Beckett and "Come in," Ellmann, p. 662. (The details of this story are at present, however, in some doubt.) For further important discussions of the state of the text, see Jack P. Dalton and Clive Hart, eds., *Twelve and a Tilly: Essays on the Occasion of the 25th Anniversary of Finnegans Wake* (London: Faber & Faber, 1966), pp. 119-37.

48. Jack P. Dalton, "Kiswahili Words in *Finnegans Wake*," to appear shortly in *A Wake Digest*, ed. Clive Hart and Fritz Senn.

49. "Corrections of Misprints in *Finnegans Wake*" (London: Faber & Faber, 1945).

50. A. Walton Litz, *The Art of James Joyce: Method and Design in "Ulysses" and "Finnegans Wake"* (London: Oxford University Press, 1961), p. 109.

Biographical Notes

JAMES F. ATHERTON, a leading English authority on Joyce, is the author of *The Books at the Wake: A Study of Literary Allusions in James Joyce's Finnegans Wake* (Viking). He has written widely on Joyce in such journals as the *James Joyce Quarterly,* and has also provided the introduction for and otherwise contributed to the Heinemann Modern Novel Series *A Portrait of the Artist as a Young Man.*

WILLIAM BLISSETT, a native of Saskatchewan, is Professor of English in University College, University of Toronto, and editor of the University of Toronto *Quarterly*. He is a student of Renaissance literature but is also engaged in a study of Wagner's influence on the arts, of which the essay herein is the eighth section to be published. He is a frequent contributor to learned journals.

CLIVE HART is at present Associate Professor of English at the University of Newcastle, New South Wales. He has published *Structure and Motif in Finnegans Wake* (Northwestern University Press) and *A Concordance to Finnegans Wake* (Minnesota University Press), and is co-editor, with Fritz Senn, of *A Wake Newslitter.*

HERBERT HOWARTH, Associate Professor of English at the University of Pennsylvania, has written *The Irish Writers* (Hill and Wang) and *Notes on Some Figures Behind T. S. Eliot* (Houghton, Mifflin). He is doing further research and writing as a Guggenheim Fellow, 1966-67.

RICHARD M. KAIN is a Professor of English at the University of Louisville, and is the author of the four books on Joyce and modern Irish literature; he has contributed to recent commemorative

Biographical Notes

volumes on Yeats and Joyce, among them *W. B. Yeats* (Ibadan), *Irish Renaissance* (Dublin), and *Twelve and a Tilly* (London).

ROBERT GLYNN KELLY, Professor of English at Indiana University, has written literary criticism, fiction (including a novel, *A Lament for Barney Stone,* Holt, Rinehart, and Winston, 1961), and an opera libretto (*The Darkened City,* 1963). He has contributed to a variety of scholarly journals, lectures widely, and has been the recipient of the Lieber Award for excellence in teaching.

REVEREND WILLIAM T. NOON, S.J., is Professor of English at Le Moyne College, Syracuse, New York. He has published *Joyce and Aquinas* (Yale University Press) and *Poetry and Prayer* (Rutgers University Press), and has written widely on Joyce in *PMLA*, the *James Joyce Quarterly,* and other scholarly journals.

THOMAS F. STALEY, the general editor of this volume, is Assistant Professor of English at the University of Tulsa, editor of the *James Joyce Quarterly,* author of forthcoming volumes in the Twayne Series on Dorothy Richardson and Italo Svevo, and contributor to numerous periodicals of English and comparative literature. He is at present a Fulbright research scholar in Trieste, Italy.